CAREER SHOCK

James C. Cotham, III

JM Productions

P.O. BOX 1911 • BRENTWOOD, TN 37024-1911

ISBN: 0-939298-63-5

Printed in the United States of America

DEDICATION

Where I am in my career, and I'm glad to be there, is largely due to the support, encouragement, patience, and understanding of the women in my life: Rachel, who has put up with me since the beginning while I have searched for career fulfillment and have explored spiritual meaning in life's journey; our two daughters, Sara Blane and Susan Elizabeth, whom God blessed us with; my mother, who never gave up on me during the crucial teen years; and my mother-in-law, who has been a good one.

JCC
Spring, 1988

PUBLISHER'S NOTE

The practical experience of an author affects his credibility when he writes a "how-to" book. The reader may justifiably ask, "Has the writer experienced what he writes about ... or, does he write from a vague, theoretical framework?" In other words, the reader wants to know if the author offers practical help or lofty advice.

James Cotham is not a person who is unscathed by workplace reality. He has been "on the firing line" in five industries that have undergone wrenching changes during the past decade. Out of that wealth of experience — plus a broad academic background — he brings a wise and challenging approach to the area of career management.

For employees who are dissatisfied with their present work, for college students preparing for tomorrow's job market, for career beginners who want to know how to plan their career path, and for those people who somewhere along the career path became bewildered and lost their way, *Career Shock* provides essential insight and the challenge for each person to take charge of personal career planning.

CONTENTS

ACKNOWLEDGEMENTS

E. M. Forster wrote, "I suggest that the only books that influence us are those for which we are ready, and which have gone a little farther down any particular path than we have yet gone ourselves." In this context, this book was written. *Career Shock* is my responsibility but has been strengthened by many intellectual contributions, large and small, from several people whose judgment and insight I respect and trust very much.

At the top of the list are Wilson Burton, entrepreneur, sportsman, churchman, and former magazine executive and Dean Smith, who, after a full career with AT&T, has embarked on a second one in business. These friends spent an enormous amount of time mulling over my manuscript, helping immensely, both editorially and conceptually.

Several others of all ages and career stages, including executives, managers, professionals, teachers, and students provided invaluable assistance by reading the material and giving me constructive advice. These include Dr. Herbert Gabhart, Don Caldwell, David Tiller, Lynée Minor, Gene Heflin, Mark Petty, Don Sheldon, Pete Lutz, and Bill Mitchum.

Patiently pounding the word processor through numerous drafts, while offering encouragement to press on, was Carol Dunn, a very special Christian person. Assisting Carol in typing and proofreading were Nancy Rainey, Rhonda Lowe, Paula Nelson, Jan Johnson, Vernona Elliott, and Karleen Rogers.

Encouragement to write the book came from my long-time friend, Dr. John Ishee, psychologist, counselor, minister, author, and publisher. His continued support and commitment to the project is especially appreciated.

Finally, without the assistance and cooperation of Dr. Bill Troutt, president, and Dr. Wayne Brown, business school dean, both of Belmont College, this book would not have been possible. To each of the above and to Pastor Jimmy Terry, my spiritual brother, you have my heartfelt gratitude for all you did to make my dream a reality.

Jim Cotham
Nashville, Tennessee

WHAT IS CAREER SHOCK?

CAREER SHOCK ... is not having a job, not liking the one you have, feeling pressure to move elsewhere, or dreaming of greener pastures.

CAREER SHOCK ... is discovering that your journey to personal growth, material well-being, and job success (career expectations) has taken you down a road filled with unanticipated potholes, detours, and dead ends (workplace reality).

CAREER SHOCK ... is that empty, gnawing feeling in the pit of your stomach when workplace reality begins to dawn — you've lost your bearing, but you are not prepared to deal with the situation.

CAREER SHOCK ... is feeling alone in your job dilemma and not knowing where to turn or what to do next.

CAREER SHOCK ... is realizing that no one but you is looking after your career interests — that when the chips are down, few people really care.

CAREER SHOCK ... is what happens to you when you have not been a good manager of your career. You don't have your own game plan. You have never accepted the personal responsibility of taking charge of your own destiny.

CAREER SHOCK ... is this book, which will help you prevent, overcome, and survive all the above.

PART I

FACING CHANGE —

TAKING CHARGE

What is the difference between an unemployment statistic, a tragedy, and a personal catastrophe? When 10,000 people you don't know in an industry you have no connection with lose their jobs, it's a statistic. When your friend loses his job, it's a tragedy. When you lose yours, it's a catastrophe.

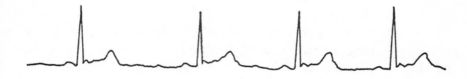

1

YOU ARE ALL YOU HAVE

When it comes to taking care of your career, you are absolutely alone and on your own. The key to career survival and growth during the turbulent 1990's is accepting responsibility for your personal well-being. Manage yourself wisely...live with meaning.

Thousands of Americans are struggling with the new and growing concern of job instability and career uncertainty. Employees from secretaries to executives are asking pressing questions:

"Is my career assured?"

"Can I count on my employer for future job security?"

"Should I change jobs for further personal growth and professional development?"

"How do I go about finding a good job with career potential?"

"When it comes to my career, whom can I trust?"

"How can I find true success and happiness in my work life?"

Some people make the decision to change jobs or evaluate their careers but lack effective follow through. They have good motives but don't have a plan. Still others, and the number is increasing, have had the job change decision made for them. With little warning, they have been terminated. Set adrift, they are in the lonely search for new employment. They seek peace of mind and a fresh sense of direction in life, but they don't know how to go about achieving it.

"CAREER SHOCK"

Informal discussions with scores of people caught up in career problems—young and old, including managers, teachers, professionals, and clerical workers—have led me to an alarming conclusion. *Most people suddenly facing the need to change jobs or redirect their careers experience what I call "career shock."*

Drifting along year to year, they have taken little or no initiative to take steps required to make their career happen *for* them. Instead, they have simply wandered through life letting their careers happen *to* them. When questioned about who is in charge of their careers or who is really looking after their interests at work, few have good answers. They just assume somebody else is.

Suddenly faced with not having a job or with wanting to move elsewhere, seeking greener pastures, they discover their reasoning is false. No one is there to pave the way to new employment. Reality begins to dawn. They realize for the first time they are alone and on their own in their search. But knowing neither where to turn nor understanding what steps to take, they have difficulty coming to grips with their dilemma. Their chief concern is very basic: "What should I do next?"

UNSHACKLE THE BONDS

What many people don't realize is that job security and career growth are the sole responsibility of the individual, not the corporation or the employer. Most people, regardless of career stage, make the fundamental mistake of depending on others rather than themselves to make good things happen. They have shirked responsibility for their economic well-being and simply have never taken charge of their own careers. Now, surprised by an unfortunate turn of events, they are in trouble. I grieve for those who despise their jobs, who experience stress and frustration at work, who are unhappy or feel uneasy about their present and future outlooks, or who endure economic hardship and emotional strain because of career problems—yet do nothing to unshackle the bonds. I dedicate this book to them with the hope that they will wake up, quit depending on others, and accept full accountability for themselves.

BE ALERT TO FUTURE TRENDS

America is experiencing a transformation more dramatic than the Industrial Revolution of the 19th century that will be marked by job upheaval and mass firings in the business sector during the remaining years of the 20th century. No industry, profession, or public institution will be immune to this traumatic economic and technological renaissance now underway.

You, whether an executive, a factory worker or anything in between, must understand what is happening and take steps necessary to prevent unpleasant consequences of career shock. Set a goal to benefit from career opportunities in the new "post-industrial" or "information age" economy now emerging and to avoid being victimized by the coming turbulence of the 1990's. You must make a personal action plan to minimize career threats and maximize personal growth.

Attitude is the first hurdle to overcome. Develop a new state of mind about yourself. Define a philosophy of life to guide you. Fully understand what you stand for ethically and morally as a human being. Dealing with these issues on a deep intellectural level will get you going in the right direction.

WHAT IS MY INTEREST?

During a 30-year career, I have gone through (and survived) several job changes, some of which included extensive career redirection. Having held executive positions in five industries experiencing dramatic restructuring—energy, telecommunications, banking, higher education, and government—I have lived first-hand much of the anxiety felt by thousands of employees concerned about the future of their employer and overall direction of the American economy.

Because of my own job experiences, I have stepped inside the shoes of those grappling with career problems and employment searches. I know the impact of career change on self-esteem, financial security, and family relations.

Please understand that I am not in the career counseling business. But because of my personal background, coupled with having held several "high visibility" positions, people concerned about their careers are constantly referred to me just to talk. They come on a regular basis to seek advice.

I've discovered that most people, when faced with a personal job crisis, either are "winging it" by reading books on writing resumés, finding a job, or other superficial "one minute" solutions that pervade our "quick fix" society. But they are starting at the wrong place. Feeling very uncomfortable, with family obligations, financial commitments, and perhaps a bruised ego, they seek relief and want it soon. I try to get them thinking about finding opportunity, not solving problems.

As a starting place, I tell of my own career experiences: about why I changed, about how I arrived at my conclusion to move on, about steps taken to implement my decision, and about how I felt concerning my actions later. Were there repercussions for my family? And looking back, did I have any regrets? This conversation lets them know others have faced the same problems and experienced similar stress.

Nearly everyone with whom I visit takes a keen interest in my responses. Details of my career decisions sometimes give encouragement and self-assurance. When I discuss my mistakes, and I've made a few, it serves as a checklist of warnings many have never considered.

WHAT I'VE LOOKED FOR IN JOBS

I've always demanded seven qualities in a job:

1. Belief in the organization's goals and purposes and how management is achieving them.

2. Executive leadership I respect.

3. An ample opportunity to use my skills and talents.

4. Intellectual stimulation and growth.

5. A chance to make a real contribution.

6. The ability to have fun and enjoy my work.

7. Quality time available for family.

If any one of these seven qualities was not present or possible, I moved on. Much to my wife's chagrin, money has never been top priority. Quite frankly, if my income for the past 15 years were plotted on a graph, it would look like a roller coaster.

With friends scratching their heads in disbelief, I've walked away from jobs that, from the outside, looked as though they had everything:

fancy title, big car with telephone, expense account, country club membership, authority, and status. The problem was, at some point, each position didn't meet all seven quality standards I have set for myself. Justifying myself to peers or being concerned about what others thought has never been a problem for me. In fact, several friends and associates have commented they wish they had the nerve to break away from their current circumstances. Sadly, most never do.

LIVE YOUR CONVICTIONS

The secret to evaluating career status and progress is to approach the issue philosophically from within yourself. My goal in measuring the value of jobs is not to be trapped by positions that, because of prestige, material considerations, or peer approval, feed my ego but starve my spirit. This approach to career management requires a solid understanding of what is going on inside yourself, what you stand for, knowing what is important in terms of fundamental beliefs and basic values, having a strong faith spiritually coupled with courage to rely on that faith, and exercising self-discipline to live your convictions.

This hard-nosed philosophy has prevented much unnecessary unhappiness, futile agonizing, and wasted effort over a career that began in 1957. In fact, because I have taken the time to carefully think through these issues and deal with them on a personal level, I've lived an exciting 30-year adventure. My experiences have been rewarding all the way.

SYMPTOMS OF CAREER SHOCK

Most people experiencing career shock share many similar feelings: burnout, stress, boredom, disappointment, and unhappiness. Some say they have stayed with the same organization too long. They feel stale and unchallenged. Others sense a dead end in their job and see little hope, real or imagined, for advancement or achievement. Attitudes are often expressed in these terms: dissatisfaction, insecurity, frustration, conflict, or financial pressures. Some talk pointedly about hopelessness, betrayal, and anger.

Most people have three characteristics in common: they don't fully understand what has happened in their career or why; they don't know what is really going on inside themselves (their values, beliefs, and priorities); and they don't have the makings of a game plan to guide them out of their problem. With no sense of direction, they are stumbling through one of the most critical times of their lives and are being victimized by the experience.

BEWARE OF BLACK MAGIC

Another common thread is that people let their current situation sneak up on them. Overly dependent on employers for job growth, career advancement, and personal happiness, employees are charmed into dependency and inaction by what I call "corporate seduction" and "corporate voodoo." Corporate seduction, beginning with the hiring process, promises young people careers, perks, and pensions, yet dumps them out on the street in ever-increasing numbers and with ever-increasing frequency.

Corporate voodoo finds its power in loyalty. Management preaches it, demands it, enforces it, but seldom delivers it.

Employees under the spell of corporate black magic exist in a state of self-paralysis, unable to resist these lures or face the need to change. They remain frozen to the present.

Or, heavily in debt, locked into the grasp of peer relationships, or never having really taken charge of anything, employees can't bring themselves to cut the ties binding them to existing circumstances. They haven't taken decisive steps on their own initiative to make the right things happen for them. Many aren't even sure what the right things are.

Corporate black magic is so prevalent in the American workplace today that identifying and dealing with it will be discussed in more detail in Chapter Seven.

BUSY-NESS OR BUSINESS

Most people having to deal with job change or career assessment have good intentions. The problem is that these desires are neither supported by specific goals nor reinforced by useful follow-through. Instead, workers are caught up in life's daily "busy-ness," ignoring career "business." Working day-to- day, complaining about their frustrations, daydreaming about the future, hoping something good will happen, experiencing sleepless nights, exhausting emotional energy, and draining their spirit, they always mean to live. Somehow, they unwittingly substitute this unproductive activity for gutsy steps and decisive actions required to live with meaning.

SPECIAL CONCERN FOR CAREER BEGINNERS

My first 18 years were spent in higher education as university professor, research economist, executive development program director, and business school associate dean. These assignments allowed me to work closely with thousands of young people as teacher, advisor, confessor, and career counselor. Since those days, I've made it my business to keep up with economic developments, employment trends, and career patterns in this country.

I especially worry about career beginners: college students preparing to enter the world of work, single parent breadwinners, spouses, and others finding it imperative to enter the work force for the first time, regardless of age. My fear is this: Is the workplace changing faster than counseling and direction given to career beginners? Have we been guided by too much outdated, conventional wisdom regarding the future of our economy or job market developing for the 1990's? Do we live in the past? The bottom line question is this: Are today's young people getting yesterday's advice about tomorrow's jobs? The implications are frightening to contemplate.

MANAGE YOURSELF WISELY

As a career-minded worker, keep yourself on a path in tune with your hopes and dreams. I challenge you in five areas:

1. Be alert to career-threatening problems and career-advancing opportunities in your industry or profession. Do homework. Don't be outdated in your thinking. Ask tough questions at work. Do not be charmed by supervisors into a sense of false security and inaction. Look beyond your employer to trade associations and professional organiza-

tions for information. Be alert to signs, signals, and trends indicating future changes and new directions.

2. Periodically assess technical skills and employment strengths. Evaluate present job circumstances. Review career objectives. Be candid about yourself. Are you on track?

3. Then, based on what is important, coupled with what you realistically have to offer employers, do whatever is required to achieve your career goals to the fullest.

4. Take charge! Have faith and confidence in yourself. Show courage of conviction. Demonstrate self-discipline. Position yourself always to operate on your initiative and on your timetable. Make your career work for you. Never count on any single person or organization to look after career interests or to assure success. The stakes are too high. Whatever the cost, don't become vulnerable to the whims of others or the pressure of peers. Accept leadership responsibility for all career-related action and follow-through.

5. When it comes to your job and career, you are absolutely alone and on your own. Never forget this fundamental career management principle. Turn the thought of being alone and having to accept self-dependency into your competitive edge. By so doing, you will quickly get ahead of others who live in a state of paralysis and who can't accept personal responsibility for their own career planning. The question then becomes: Where do I go from here?

SELF-MANAGEMENT

The key to career survival and personal growth in America's impersonal workplace of tomorrow can be found in the principles of self-reliance and self-management..."To thine own self be true." However, I must make myself quite clear on the subject. I am not promoting the popular ethic of "me-ism," the "if-it-feels-good-do-it" approach in life. This is self-reliance carried to a negative extreme.

Nor do I mean a total relying on self, as in secular humanism. I mean just the opposite. The self-management I embrace advocates getting out of the grasp of others and resisting peer pressure. This self-management depends on more than intellect and understanding: it relies on solid beliefs and values, and on developing spiritual maturity. Become thoughtful about what is important in life and accept full responsibility, as an adult, for your own economic and moral well-being. These are major steps to becoming a self-manager.

MAKING CRUCIAL LIFE DECISIONS

While this book concentrates on job and career topics, the principles are also helpful in developing personal guidelines for total living. The two can't be separated.

As a career seeker, your personal challenge is clear. You must fully accept the burden of sizing up your job situation and career outlook as both exist today and determine the direction in which each is likely to go. Then take all steps required to preserve, protect, and promote career potential.

Every individual (and that means you) must take total responsibility, and accept personal accountability through self- management, for five crucial life decisions:

1. Decide specifically what you want out of your career. Write it down. Focus on three-year cycles (see Appendix for specific details on three-year career reviews). Deal with this short planning period because there are too many uncertainties beyond three years. Your interests may change. New opportunities might crop up. Unforseeable circumstances could occur. The key is to be prepared. Don't be caught off guard.

2. Identify specific avenues for obtaining objectives. Do your homework. Read. Listen. Ask questions. Find out what's happening and why.

3. Deal with reality. Be totally honest with yourself. What do you have to offer in the job marketplace? What will it take to develop competitive employment skills? Determine specific actions and commitments required of you.

4. Resolve these tough questions: "Will career success as I seek it also bring true, inner happiness?" "Do I really understand what drives me emotionally?" Separate your ego needs and spiritual needs to check whether your ambitions are grounded in solid principles. This has to do with such issues as psychological motivations, personal maturity, peer pressure, emotional stability, ethical standards, basic beliefs, and spiritual values.

5. Whatever your answers to these questions, come to grips with and implement your career decisions. Be forceful. Don't shrink from

this responsibility. Don't rationalize or compromise. Don't wait for someone to step in and do the work. Postponing action only delays the inevitable. Do what you must to minimize the pain of anxiety and uncertainty.

SUSTAIN YOUR PACE

Sooner or later, everyone must find a "sustained" level of goal-directed work that involves, motivates, excites, challenges, and fulfills inner needs. Otherwise, life is destined to be a series of frustrations, setbacks, and disappointments.

In my own life, I have set career goals and have done what is demanded educationally, professionally, and in conducting my personal affairs to be successful by my own measures. At all costs, I have protected my self-worth, personal dignity, and reputation. Sometimes the short-term consequences have been painful to me and my family because of the decisions I've had to make to preserve these principles, but after 30 years I am proud of the achievement. My family understands and respects me. Looking back, I have discovered that prayer and church attendance have helped immeasurably during the difficult times.

KEY TO SELF-CONFIDENCE

The real secret to self-confidence is to develop basic beliefs and spiritual values as the undergirding support throughout a lifelong search for career success and personal achievement. Several years ago, I discovered the power of spirituality and what relying on biblically based principles to provide counsel, support, and encouragement can mean. Because of this unwavering source of inner strength, life for me has taken on deeper meaning and has become a spiritual walk. I am now much more self-confident in what I do and in how I earn my living. Most importantly, I am at peace with myself. And the feeling is great!

It is in this context, motivated by career experiences, knowing how I feel about myself, and better understanding the source of my own inner strength as I go through life, that this book was written. I hope the ideas and recommendations help my readers on their career journeys.

GETTING STARTED CHECKLIST

- Confirm your present career path and be committed to it, or begin now to seek new destinations.
- Don't maintain yourself in a destructive state of self- paralysis.
- Get off dead center and do something positive.
- Get going by taking charge.
- Remember that you are all you have.

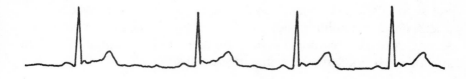

2

TAKE CHARGE NOW!

Do you think you are immune from job upheaval in America's workplace? That you have job security? Guaranteed promotions? Pay increases? Perks? If so, your problem is worse than most. The reason? You don't know you have a problem.

From large corporations to small businesses, America's employers are retooling, modernizing, reorganizing, regrouping, rethinking, downsizing, selling out, bailing out, going under, waiting and watching, or doing nothing.

One thing is for certain — the national economy is undergoing an unparalleled overhaul, changing the way we live, work, and do business. New methods, procedures, and techniques are being introduced on the assembly line, and in the office, at a staggering rate. Employees, especially those who do nothing to stay prepared, will suffer "obsolescence shock" from outdated job skills in the years ahead.

UPHEAVAL IN THE WORKPLACE

Very complex factors are fueling unprecedented workplace turmoil in America: emerging computer-based technologies in manufacturing, health care, and communications; aggressive worldwide competition; heightening trade tensions; deregulation in transportation, telecommunications, and banking; corporate mergers, acquisitions, divestitures; increased uncertainty in third world economies; burgeoning small-business start-ups; tightening accountability for malpractice;

upward cost trends in medical care; toughening management leadership styles; population shifts and new demographic patterns; gyrations in oil prices; uncertain public policy about government deficits, tax structure, and interest rates; confusion about fundamentals of capital formation and job creation; and wild swings in the stock market.

WALL STREET MANIA

Don't forget Wall Street. In the wake of Black Monday, 1987, shareholders are applying tremendous pressure to produce stronger earnings, maximize stock prices, and increase dividend yields. If the fuse of patience for quick financial gain in the stock market was burning short before the crash of 1987, witness the explosion of corporate restructuring now going on to recoup losses. In response, management attitudes toward employees are changing dramatically. Everyone from board members to senior executives, to middle managers, to supervisors, and to workers at all levels are feeling the pressure for better operating results.

In response, companies are pushed to cut operating costs, introduce new techniques, reduce payroll costs and cut employees as a means for increased profitability. That's why machines are replacing people and jobs are being eliminated, redefined, and consolidated in record numbers. Because of increased pressure on management, there is less forgiveness down through the ranks for mistakes of judgment. This leads to the uncertainty, insecurity, and instability overtaking the workplace. And there is little immunity. White collar and blue collar workers alike have been hit hard by the workplace revolution underway.

DO YOU STILL NEED CONVINCING?

If these reasons are not convincing of the widespread job instability and growing career uncertainty, then bear in mind that various projections indicate several million manufacturing and service industry jobs will have their content altered dramatically as the 1990's close. Many jobs will be eliminated. *The reason?* Technology and change! This large employee group will have to be retrained. These displaced workers will make job market competition stiffen when they re-enter.

Don't misunderstand. There will be plenty of work. The catch is, skills needed to compete for tomorrow's better jobs will be vastly different and more complex than in the past. The key to finding a good paying job with meaty content and challenge will be to have the new skills required.

Also keep in mind that 75 percent of today's workers, white collar and blue collar, factory and office, will still be in the labor force by the year 2000. Changing demographics will add confusion. People are living and working longer. Many will have insufficient financial means needed to retire and live a life of dignity. More people will enter the labor force in mid-life, particularly women. The rate of new job openings caused by natural attrition and changing retirement rules will be a key indication of employment potential. Unsettling statistics and news headlines could suddenly become a personal crisis. Think about it.

WHERE DOES THIS LEAVE EMPLOYEES?

Unfortunately, until trade, budget deficit, and technology issues can be resolved and a new sense of economic stability established, many people will have been left holding the bag. For those seeking a fresh perspective about the future, employment forecasts and hiring trends are increasingly unclear. The country's demographics are changing drastically. Our population is aging. We are moving from the "baby boom" generation to the "baby bust" era. People are living longer, raising new questions about pension plans, time utilization, health care, and the quality of life during retirement. Throughout the 1990's, there will be fewer young workers available to work and more people 65 and older needing jobs.

Compared to the 1960's, 1970's, and early 1980's, the demand for college graduates will be uneven, both in terms of necessary skills and job location. The need for basic, entry-level skills, particularly for 18-year olds, will be enormous. The question is: Will young people have the specific technical skills and assume the responsibility required?

Up to 90 percent of all jobs created through the 1990's will be in service industries. Some will be high-paying, with solid content and good career potential such as insurance, banking, computers, and health sciences. But many will be near minimum wage levels with little challenge and low career appeal. Some jobs will be downright boring. From

80 to 90 percent of all new jobs will be located in major metropolitan areas. Many small towns and most rural areas will be in serious trouble.

DON'T BE AN OSTRICH

Many workers now on the bone pile of unemployment, forced career change, and reduced standard of living have been caught by surprise and are asking: *"What happened?"*

Others saw their demise coming but either denied reality or didn't have the courage or wisdom to do anything about it. They just *"let it happen."*

Still others felt protected from changes and said, *"It won't happen."* But it did.

And there were those who quietly inquired, *"Will it happen?"* but were assured by Pinocchio-like managers and corporate medicine men that everything was great, even right up to the day *"it did happen"* ... and their pink slip was issued. Unfortunately, this seamy side of the job reorganization movement is happening with increasing frequency.

Do not hide like an ostrich and hope the problem of a churning, unstable economy will go away. Instead, be like those who saw it coming, were prepared, were courageous, faced their dilemma head on, did something positive, and saved their lifestyles through individual effort.

YOU HAVE BEEN FOREWARNED!

If you let something bad happen to you, it's your own fault. Don't end up a statistic in a news story or experience a personal calamity. Remember, no industry, company, non-profit organization, educational institution, or government agency of any kind, at any level, anywhere, is totally protected from the changes now taking place and those yet to come.

That means no occupation, profession, job skill, or existing employment classification is totally home free. It's entirely up to you to face the music. Read the signs and interpret the signals indicating new trends and different directions in your industry or profession.

Begin right now to determine where you stand. Ask yourself, *"Am*

I vulnerable? Do I have what it takes to produce? Am I willing to commit what it takes? Will I have the opportunity to deliver? Do I need to take steps to protect my future? Should I make the move now to preserve my career?"

GOOD NEWS — BAD NEWS

There is hope! But the future is filled with fog. The painful price of lifting it will be paid in technical skills development, financial flexibility, and personal mobility. The good news is that analysts are projecting exciting new career opportunities in the post-renaissance job market of the 1990's and beyond. A dramatic economic and technological transformation, such as the one now being experienced, will ultimately create more new jobs than are being lost. This is one of the positive lessons of history. Count on it.

Young people, properly prepared, can look forward to the possibility of growth, satisfaction, challenge, and career fulfillment over the long haul. In fact, opportunities will never be greater for those who possess the specific technical and decision skills needed, demonstrate determination in locating available jobs, have the mobility to relocate, and possess the financial means to get there.

The bad news is that as technology moves forward and ground rules change, more and more individuals of all ages will enter the gray area of skills obsolescence and workplace instability. Uninformed, insecure, mentally lazy, overconfident, or paralyzed by current success, these people will be like fish deprived of oxygen — they will soon bloat and die. Do not be stifled by career circumstances or hoodwinked by cockiness. Do not be included in this kill.

What am I saying? There are employment alternatives and fresh opportunities available for development and growth, but only for effective self-managers willing to pay the price and overcome reluctance to change.

NEW FOCUS ON PEOPLE

There's more good news. One dominant prediction stands out as America moves from merger mania and the smokestack era into what has been called the "post-industrial" age, "information age," or "service economy." Expect a major reawakening regarding the value of people in the equation of profits and bottomline results. The reason? Survival! Smart leaders will come to recognize people as the key to their success and will use this new discovery to a competitive advantage.

Successful companies will again recognize that human capital, people leadership, and improved quality of life in the workplace are as crucial as investments in plant and technology. The existing problem is that the role, value, utilization, and needs of people have taken a back seat to financial, quantitative, and technical issues. This travesty has been perpetuated too long by people who think the answer to business success can be found in technical methods, financial models, and cash management practices.

In far too many organizations, people are under-valued, under-trained, under-equipped, under-skilled, under-appreciated, under-utilized, and under-led. But a major transition in leadership style will be forthcoming soon to match the structural and organizational changes now taking place in corporate America. Workers prepared with tomorrow's skills who can land jobs with employers that value people as top priority will clearly be the winners. Count on this and take heart.

Be ready to capitalize on opportunity. Maintain skills to remain valuable to employers. We know and accept that machines, computers, and automobiles can become outdated and wear out. But what about ourselves? Can a human being become obsolete as well? Unfortunately, the answer is a big "Yes" — by not keeping up with the specific skills needed. Personal attitudes about jobs also change. Enthusiasm wanes. Boredom dims excitement. Burnout can occur, so this leads to despair and giving up. All are symptoms of "obsolescence shock." Ultimately, it is up to the individual to do whatever is required to keep the pace. Get out in front of changes that inevitably take place in a dynamic workplace and put them to work.

WHAT'S THE ANSWER?

The answer is painfully simple!

Take control of the future. Put together a personal strategic plan and specific timetable for conducting self-reviews and self-assessments, and taking appropriate actions. Focus on three-year steps. Do not bog down with forecasts beyond three years. No one knows for sure what the future holds. Anything beyond three years will take care of itself, except for financial planning. If you plan aggressively in clear three-year increments, the future will work better for you.

The sad truth is that bosses, human resources people, and colleagues are not looking out for anyone else's best interests. Bosses come and go. Personnel professionals have little clout. They have been inundated for years with federal and state regulations, wage/hour rules, and EEOC requirements. Bogged down with reports, payrolls, employee complaints, and union matters, many personnel managers have become second-class citizens. But even more importantly, because financial and technical managers are in control, little if any time remains for dealing with people.

The key to success in tomorrow's workplace is self-evaluation, self-confidence, and self-reliance! But there's more: self- preservation! Self-planning! Self-preparation! Self-initiative! Self-discipline! All are required. In a word, self-management.

Whatever the circumstances, have no self-doubt or self-pity about the present or the past. Turn liabilities into assets. Turn your back on bad situations. Have courage to get started with a fresh outlook and new vision. Be willing to take risks. Be an entrepreneur when it comes to self-managing. Take the first step. Take it firmly, courageously, and with resolve. Do it immediately.

STICK TO THE BASICS

Success in this atmosphere of uncertainty will require five things of all job seekers:

1. Timely information about job availability;
2. Financial flexibility to move from job to job;
3. Family mobility to get there;
4. Guts to make the move; and
5. Sufficient skills to compete, once at the hiring desk.

No one will have guaranteed job security or career success — only opportunity to compete for available jobs. Career achievement and progress will require taking full responsibility for moral and spiritual character, career assessment, life goals, and the price of reaching your desired destination.

Career beginners, regardless of age, sex, or skills, will have to be especially alert to employment trends and stay on top of specific jobs available, where they are located, and if they can be counted on to last. Make absolutely sure training or job experience will pay off for you later.

But having a carefully developed strategic plan for career growth isn't enough. Crucial to success are two more steps. First, muster the courage to get started in a self-management program. Second, develop the stamina and discipline necessary to keep it up. It is much easier to plan and talk about what you intend to do than actually to do it. Most of us are pros at postponing. Having good intentions, we get started. But, like many people who start on a diet or exercise program, we backslide after a few weeks.

The acid test comes with taking specific actions and maintaining a sustainable pace of development. The bottom line is that when workers stop honing and sharpening skills, they lose staying power. Corporate hiring and retention policies change so quickly that most people will have to step up skills development efforts just to keep even.

There's one fundamental rule: The times demand excellence. Don't forget this. Gear your personal career strategy to excellence, then deliver excellence. Growth in the workplace under these conditions means having determination, working smarter, and doing something different to break out of the crowd. Excellence requires self-insight, self-review, self-initiative, and courage.

The secret is to do whatever is necessary to make a career happen *for* you — not *to* you. Put your hand on the throttle and take full control over existing job circumstances and career aspirations.

In a world of growing uncertainty, insecurity, and instability, the need to develop basic beliefs, to draw on spiritual guidance, and to secure the comfort of inner peace as the undergirding force in one's life has never been more vital.

TAKING CHARGE CHECKLIST

- Act now. Don't wait for things to get better somehow.
- Take charge. Don't depend on anyone else for positive action.
- Be responsible. Don't fault others or blame bad circumstances.
- Stay current. Don't dwell on history or depend on past momentum.
- Be thorough. Take all steps necessary to secure your future, however costly or painful to your daily routine and lifestyle.
- Explore. Seek new opportunities for career growth.
- Be optimistic. Become your own cheerleader and ambassador.
- Make the commitment. Take full command of your destiny.

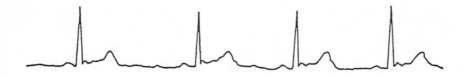

3

LEAVING THE
GARDEN OF EDEN

*"New ages are born so quietly the majority of people are
not aware of what is happening."*

— *Bishop Gerald Kennedy*

Since 1950, Americans have been living in a "fool's paradise." This predicament is more than a failure of business leadership. Business, government, labor, churches, public institutions, and individuals all share the blame by failing to realize that this world is ours to enjoy for only a fleeting moment, and that there is a stewardship responsibility to future generations. Resources are limited. America must rediscover this fundamental truth and rearrange priorities accordingly.

LIVING IN THE PROMISED LAND

Many Americans have the comforting delusion that they are in a promised land of perpetual prosperity and everlasting abundance. Most people devote efforts to living for today. In pursuing this short-sighted approach, the future is left to fend for itself.

There is a popular idea that America is blessed from above with a divine destiny. But as former Colorado Governor Richard Lamm wrote, "God didn't turn out to be any more of an American than he was English,

French, Roman, Greek, or Egyptian." In His eye, Americans are nothing special as a country or society of people. Ignoring history is a failure to realize that civilizations are not forever. They all rise and fall.

Whether it can be best described as a fool's paradise or as a "modern day Garden of Eden," the decades since World War II have been a time of unparalleled economic growth and achievement in America. It matured as an industrial nation of innovators, builders, inventors, and doers. It blossomed into a society of advertising-driven "conspicuous consumers" and pleasure seekers. Cutting-edge technologies and enormous material wealth made life easy. Americans became spoiled.

Spurred on by a proud 200 year tradition of trailblazing, frontier conquering, barnraising, and yankee ingenuity, the country developed an infallible "can't fail" attitude. The economy was fueled by seemingly endless cheap energy and funded by plenty of money and easy credit. Blessed with boundless raw materials, foodstuffs, and a generous heart, Americans committed to care for those who couldn't care for themselves and provided the promise of a secure retirement for all.

ONE MINUTE ANSWERS AND SELF-GRATIFICATION

Preoccupation with today's pleasures has obscured tomorrow's problems. The society wants to live, have fun, and enjoy. "One minute" answers and "quick fix" solutions pervade an impatient public that wants government off its back as long as someone else pays the price. It becomes a case of righteous indignation when someone or some institution goes too far over the ethical line. But self-justification sets in. The pendulum of acceptable behavior always swings back, and the range of what goes and what doesn't go seems to get wider and wider.

The self-gratification era is the environment in which nearly 60 percent of all Americans alive today grew up. Having been born since 1950, all they know is relative prosperity, either to enjoy or aspire toward. But the fact is that the Garden of Eden mentality has dulled the competitive edge needed to support economic growth and feed material prosperity. It is a painful lesson to ignore history. As former Labor Secretary Bill Brock laments, Americans become "fat, sloppy, and unproductive."

CAN THE WELL RUN DRY?

Short-sighted in our vision, we have taken for granted our sources of national economic prosperity and personal material well-being. But events since the 1970's, rooted in international energy shortages and economic recession, began to undercut national promises and commitments made to ourselves. Obligations to others around the globe have far exceeded America's capacity to deliver. But not many seem to notice the warning signs and fewer care. Reflecting the attitudes of society at large, politicians live from election to election, motivated by survival instincts and personal self-interest.

Now it's sinking in slowly and painfully that we don't live in a land of perpetual prosperity; that precious resources are in limited supply and abundance can't be assured; that all the wastes of an industrial society can't be reclaimed and that all the garbage can't be buried; machines, highways, bridges, cities, governments, and societies, like people, really do grow old and wear out. America is learning the hard way that industrial dominance isn't guaranteed, and that other industrialized nations have the technology, product quality, and commitment to manufacturing workmanship to equal if not beat us. The nation has been challenged in the world's marketplace and is losing the war of economic superiority in many job-creating, growth industries of tomorrow.

FACING REALITY

Tough questions are now being asked. Could America lose control of its technological and industrial destiny? How is it possible that so many business organizations have suddenly lost the competitive edge of earlier years? Why is there more emphasis on current profits and financial rewards instead of the "seed corn" of research and development necessary to discover new technologies needed for tomorrow's growth?

How could this malaise happen in America? In the face of mounting social problems such as the homeless, AIDS, chemical abuse, adult illiteracy, child care for working parents, and medical care for the growing numbers of poor and elderly, is it true that limits can exist to financial care for those who need it? Has society lost its moral bearings?

Could it be possible that an unhealthy imbalance between work and leisure has been reached? Does government really have to pay its debts? Is today financed by mortgaging future generations?

FAILURE OF ECONOMICS AND BUSINESS FUNDAMENTALS

Compounding the puzzle is a lack of economic policy-making con-census similar to that guiding this country for 30 postwar years. World conditions, domestic issues, and basic ground rules have changed, and economic theory as an infallible framework for decision making has fallen on hard times. Economic forecasting models and textbook concepts have failed and respect for "experts" has crumbled.

The philosophical challenge, in the most basic terms, is to discover how America can continue to fulfill its promises to the young and to the aging without putting upon its children and grandchildren an unbearable economic burden?

But in answering this question, we have no background of experience as the point of departure in clearly and accurately predicting the future. In short, as America moves into a global marketplace, there are no clear-cut prescriptions for providing the capital formation needed for economic growth. Nothing that worked in the past can be taken for granted any more. The nation is faced with obsolescence at the very core of its thinking about creating the well paying jobs needed for continued material well-being, caring for the poor and aging, and dealing with quality of life issues.

DISEASE OF ILLITERACY

America suffers from economic and educational illiteracy of epidemic proportions.

One of America's most unrecognized and misunderstood problems in Congress, corporate board rooms, and at the grass roots level is how government policies, private business decisions, and the quality of education affect capital formation, job creation, and continued economic prosperity.

It is obvious to anyone willing to look closely that the winds of economic and social change are blowing stiffly across the land. The future, just beyond the current signs of social, cultural, and economic unheaval taking place all around us, will be totally unlike the past. Because we have been liquidating our abundance and letting apathy drain our national energies, we are leaving the Garden of Eden.

There will be choices about the future. As Governor Lamm observes: "It is an iron rule of history that great nations eventually have great problems." Because changes are happening so quickly, they are difficult to absorb. But with all the economic, technical, and cultural developments underway, few of us will be able to do our jobs, handle our careers, or manage our personal affairs in the future as we have become accustomed to doing in the past and be successful at the same time.

THREATS AND CHALLENGES

We are entering an era of uncertainty in which the greatest threat to most of us will be attacks on our feeling of self-confidence, self-esteem, and self-worth. Unless we are careful, inadequate job skills, outmoded management styles, excessive government, an unpredictable economy, and outdated personal goals will sap our strength and dampen our spirit. Continued growth as an individual will require an honest examination of ourselves in terms of careers, priorities, objectives, ethics, values, commitments, and utilization of our time and talents.

COMPETITIVE EDGE

The advantage will go to those willing to seek deeper meaning about themselves, to develop a sense of direction, to use a moral compass for guidance, to demonstrate courage of conviction about their career, to accept responsibility for themselves, and to prepare for the future through self-reliance, self-awareness, and self-discipline. This will require withstanding pressure of colleagues and loyalty to peers, overcoming denial of change, allegiance to tradition, obedience to routine, and status quo, and knocking aside other obstacles to self-initiative and freedom of flexibility.

Said another way, "Blessed are those who develop a fresh sense of personal responsibility, self-preparedness, and concern for self-survival, for they surely will not be disappointed."

Every individual must make a choice as he lives daily at the edge of obsolescence and on the threshold of opportunity. One choice is to look back into the past toward Eden and long for a comfort zone that appears secure. Having an irresistible urge to feel good, you can view life through a rear view mirror, remembering the way it was. Assuming the future to be an extension of the past, you can pause and wait to see what happens. You can find excuses or, in the worst case, you can even deny the existence of changes happening in your life.

Or you can remember that "You are all you have." Step out of the pack and demonstrate personal leadership. Take command. This requires enduring the discomfort of assuming responsibility for ourselves, warding off pressures of others, and taking control of our career. Recognize the hard fact that tomorrow will be unlike yesterday. Then, by seizing opportunity, move into the future on the strengths of skill and conviction. It's a lonely decision for most.

MAKING RIGHT CHOICES

As you continue your search for growth and professional achievement, answer these six questions personally. Then carefully consider the observations that follow about major changes unfolding in today's workplace.

1. Why are Americans experiencing the dilemma of job upheaval?

2. By attitude and behavior, do I contribute to the "Garden of Eden" mentality pervading the country?

3. Do I intend to do everything in my power to prevent   career shock and job obsolescence from happening to me?

4. Will I do my part as a citizen to stay informed and accept stewardship responsibility for regaining perspective?

5. Do I remain unconvinced there is a problem?

6. Am I convinced that I'm protected from the job and career problems I see in others?

Remember this: The most serious career problems happen to those who live in the present, who assume that somebody else is taking care of their future, who are consumed by materialism or who, through fear, can't bring themselves to assume control of their own well-being. They are the ones who either don't think they have problems or can't face their problems.

PRODUCTS OF A "FOOL'S PARADISE"

• America has been in a severe management crisis since 1973. Energy prices have roller coastered. Price fixing tactics by the oil producing countries (OPEC) in the 1970's signaled the beginning of un-precedented change in our business system. But a decade later, once again temporarily losing control of oil production, the actions of OPEC have helped create a second violent new wave of economic change throughout our society. Companies, families, and individuals in the "oil patch" region of America have been hardest hit.

• The assurances of more inflation each year during two decades have masked many mistakes and have protected many poor managers. Minimum inflation during the mid-80's has blown their cover. Tough competitors in the international marketplace, lower prices for materials, supplies, and finished goods, and reduced interest rates are beginning to flush incompetence down the drain. These poor managers are being recognized as unaffordable burdens.

• America is quickly losing dominance in the world economy through lower quality products, inefficient manufacturing, a lull in crea-tive research and development, and ineffective marketing. Everyone seeks a scapegoat: management blames labor, labor blames manage-ment, big business blames government, government blames big busi-ness, America blames Japan, and Japan blames America. Stop! There's enough blame to go around. America must stop blaming and start ad-dressing the challenge of providing good jobs and career opportunities for citizens of all ages without mortgaging generations to come.

• Our country is quickly entering a new phase of high-tech economic activity. New industries of the 1990's will be grounded in sophisticated electronics, computer science, mathematics, physics, and biotechnology. Heavy industry is aging, obsolete, or just plain worn out. Some of this is due to short-sighted management and labor, some be-cause of bad government tax policy. Until new computer-driven and science-based technologies are in place, most new jobs for young and old alike will be in small businesses, particularly service industries, much of which has been characterized by noted management consultant Peter Drucker as being either "low-tech" or "no-tech" in content. This means many jobs will have little challenge, excitment, career growth potential, or long-term appeal.

• The nation is spoiled rotten. It demands more from its society than it gives. It consumes and doesn't replenish. It spends and doesn't save. No wonder it fails to reduce the national debt and has for the first time in history become a debtor nation.

• Americans have been slow to predict, recognize, and respond to technological breakthroughs and economic trends that are overtaking us. People in our country are inflexible and resist change; thus, they become victims.

• The nation is shortsighted and does not understand the implications of its decisions about using limited natural resources, burning or recycling trash, or affecting the air, land, and water with toxic waste and industrial pollution.

• Our comfort zone is broad, even foolishly complacent, and is paralyzed by routine. Focused on today and its material pleasures, it is difficult for Americans to bear the pain of preparing for tomorrow's technologies, production processes, and workplace requirements that will make the country competitive again in the global marketplace.

• Personal leadership in America is woefully outmoded. Priorities focus on short-term financial profits and ignore the future. Now the workplace is in deep distress. Uncertainty, instability, and ambiguity reign. The result of this turmoil is in coined phrases such as "executive stress," "burn out," and "job meltdown." Employees turn to drugs, alcohol, spouse abuse, divorce, and even suicide. Through employee assistance programs (EAP), corporate America says we must rehabilitate the employee. We also need Leadership Assistance programs (LAP) to rehabilitate the leadership style of corporate America.

• Why are so many high schools, colleges, and universities giving today's graduates yesterday's advice about tomorrow's opportunities? Textbooks and classroom lectures are falling behind the realities facing today's policy makers. It is becoming increasingly difficult to identify the forefront of knowledge, track the leading edge, and stay in front of change. The workplace has become the firing line.

• Public schools fail to teach tomorrow's workers how to read, write, calculate, and reason sufficiently to survive in the high-tech workplace awaiting them. But parents aren't up in arms over this tragedy unfolding right before their eyes. Who is looking after students? Have parents abandoned young people? Has the job of raising children been relegated to teachers, disc jockeys, and television producers? Is the future fending for itself?

● After observing thousands of students go from the classroom to the workplace during the last 30 years, I have one overriding conclusion about education: *There is little, if any, relationship between grades in college and success in life.* Rather than teaching young people how to think, tests are geared to scoring well. Instead, American youth must have the skills needed to survive economically, be stimulated intellectually, and grow professionally in a "high-tech" information-based society.

● Shareholders and corporate boards measure performance solely on numbers. They relentlessly demand that business performance be measured on a quarter-by-quarter and year-by-year basis. This was appropriate "yesterday" during competitive dominance, economic stability, positive business trends, marketplace predictability, and economic control. But yesterday has passed.

● The current crop of middle managers, especially those possessing MBAs, has been overly influenced by quantitative methods, resource allocation models, and financial forecasting. Business schools have focused on teaching policy level problem-solving, boardroom solutions, and executive decision-making. The human side of management has been scorned by too many corporate executives, deans, and professors. But it's not technologies, products, markets, cash management, or advertising, that ultimately make business work — it's PEOPLE! America's work force and company profits have suffered because of this incredible shortcoming.

● Managers are often chosen for the wrong reasons. Leadership responsibility at all levels is too often assigned to people who aren't capable of leading others. They don't possess the skills required to help subordinates develop their talents and reach full potential. Because someone is a good "doer" that someone may not be a good leader. We haven't learned that lousy "people-management" ultimately destroys a business. Business leadership blames everyone for these failures — except themselves.

● Too many career beginners, fresh college graduates, the

MBAs, and others, enter the job market for the first time and set goals the wrong way. They have the wrong priorities. The entire focus is on "now." Too often, success is expressed in terms of physical possessions: BMWs, condos, designer clothes, and ski trips. Reward and gratification concentrate on the present, on consumption, not on building a foundation for future financial security and career flexibility. Beginners are not thinking about how they will grow and develop. They just assume they will. Many don't.

• Yesterday, one might change jobs once or twice in a lifetime. Any more than that would be taken as instability or unrealiability. Tomorrow, it may be necessary to change five or six times to survive over a 40-year work career.

• The bottom line is this: Never forget that if you don't take care of yourself in the workplace in a businesslike manner at the beginning, always knowing where you stand, always in control, you can rest assured that somebody else will give you the business in the end.

CAREER: MILESTONES VS. MILLSTONES

Do two important things in career development and in life. First, through daily actions and day-to-day performance, write your resumé. What is done, how time and skills are used each day, will develop the ammunition (or lack of it) needed for tomorrow's job market.

Also, prepare an epitaph. The crucial questions are these: What, if anything, will be said about you at career's end? Will you make a mark in life? Will you leave your imprint? Or will your life be nothing more than smoke through a soot-filled chimney? Live in such a way that, when retirement comes, there will be no regrets. The older you get the more important this issue becomes. But you are laying the groundwork now. Use wisely the time that can't be recovered.

Life is mostly a spiritual journey: discovering who you really are, what you stand for, and how you can live with meaning. It is important to understand that the most significant measure of life's achievement cannot be cashed at the bank. Once again, ask yourself: Based on my present path in life, how will I be remembered? Is there any significance to my life? Then ask: How do I want to be remembered? What can I do to make a difference? Do what you must to fill the gap.

Far too many people wake up toward the end of their careers and realize lost potential. They wasted time and ability. Life was a series of millstones instead of milestones. They missed opportunities. Working passively, they assumed someone else was taking care of their careers. They had no plan, no initiative. They failed to take charge of their lives and to work smart while they could. Suddenly, it was too late.

They now find themselves shackled by a course of events over which control has been lost. Their opportunity for fullness in life is gone. Instead of making good things happen for them, they let bad things happen to them. They have regrets and have to live with them. Avoid this quicksand at all costs.

LET NOTHING DEFEAT YOU

- In making your plans and setting your objectives, always be careful what you wish for. Too often people set and attain the wrong goals. Living with the consequences of bad goals can be painful.
- At all costs, protect your self-worth and personal dignity. Pay whatever the price to preserve your reputation. Keep your good name.
- There are good people in workplace America. But there are some devious people who gain at other's expense, dampen spirits, and inflict others with their own emotional inadequacies and personality deficiencies. These people will take advantage of you and your talent, or warp your sense of values. Stick close to the good people. Run from the bad ones, if you can. But be able to handle them when running isn't an option.
- There are no guarantees in our competitive economic system and job market. All we have is the opportunity to rise to our potential. We have freedom to try, freedom to succeed, and freedom to fail. This is what America has been about for more than 200 years.
- There is absolutely no reason you can't excel in what you do. Strive to achieve whatever is important. Take command. Be responsible for yourself. Get started now!
- You will become a slave to whatever defeats you. Do not let people defeat you. Do not let circumstances defeat you. Most of all, do not *defeat yourself*. Do not let your vision perish!

CAREER REALITY CHECKLIST

- Never forget that in today's fast-paced, technology-driven workplace, people's job skills can quickly become outdated. People, like machines, end up on the scrap pile.
- Have a sense of urgency about your planning, your research, your decisions, and your actions. Decide what you need to be doing.
- Have the self-confidence and courage to follow through.
- Do it. You make it happen!

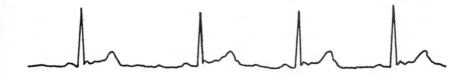

4

WILL THE FUTURE

BE FRIEND OR FOE?

Change is the common thread in the history of mankind.
It is predictable and inevitable, impersonal and relentless. The
quickening pace is touching everyone. Here's the challenge: To
be prepared to respond.

Poet-philosopher George Santayana offers some solid advice: "Those who ignore the lessons of history are doomed to repeat them." The message is to remember the past and to avoid reliving it. From a career perspective, stay ahead of others by learning the lessons of history and how the past tends to repeat itself.

To get a handle on tomorrow, go back into pages of time to understand the rise and fall of governments, societies, and civilizations over the centuries. Look closely at America's 200-year record that tracks the growth and decline of businesses, industries, and geographical regions based on changing industrial technologies, agricultural methods, population patterns, and cultural trends.

How many people have gone to work in a factory, shop, office, small retail business, non-profit organization, or government agency, thinking that they would stay employed for a lifetime, only to discover that the employer folds, that the assembly line or company suddenly isn't competitive, that markets are lost, that revenues decline, that budgets are reduced and employee levels are cut back, or that somebody bought the firm, consolidated operations, and trimmed the workforce? The answer is *millions* of people.

Pay attention to Santayana's message. Don't assume the future is secure. Avoid dedicating all thoughts, efforts, and energies to supplying current needs and enjoying today's pleasures. Conventional wisdom says the world is on a steady course and tomorrow is simply an extension of today. History proves convention wrong.

WHAT DOES THE FUTURE HOLD?

Forces often turn unnoticed on a collision course to shape profound change in new directions. Is America on the edge of a new age? Will the 1990's be a time of prosperity or a period of turbulence? One can only speculate.

Pay attention to signs and signals in your job, just as the farmer concerned about storms asks, "Are the leaves turning against the wind?" Anticipating possible changes is important to workers who make careers happen *for* them rather than *to* them. Don't go to sleep at the switch. Maintain flexibility.

THE TECHNOLOGICAL PACE IS QUICKENING

Look around at the electronic marvels in cars, kitchens, and homes. Compare today's work tools and communication methods with those used just five years ago. Consider scientific breakthroughs and technology-based inventions now taken for granted that impacted jobs, lifestyles, and economic well-being throughout the postwar period.

Since World War II, transistors, automation, atomic power, the Salk vaccine, television, lazers, microchips, microwaves, video products, satellites, superconductors and fiber optics have all been developed. Americans walked on the Moon. Even something as simple as the portable charcoal grill was the beginning of a cultural revolution. In the early 1950's, the grill gained national popularity. It brought people outdoors, changed the role of the kitchen, caused innovations in food packaging and supermarket merchandising, kept people out of restaurants, and shifted some of the cooking responsibility to the male. Now the outdoor charcoal grill is taken for granted. I was a teenager when the grill first came on the retail market. I watched it change the way my parents, along with countless others, approached hamburgers, picnics, and eating out.

Vividly described in "Marketing Myopia," industries which were once pillars of strength and power, but were lacking in flexibility and vision, have come and gone with changing technology.[1] On a larger scale, history reveals that monetary and political fortunes have been made or lost based on the ability to anticipate and manage change.

Throughout recorded time, thriving, flourishing communities and civilizations have withered and faded by becoming complacent and by drifting away from fundamental values holding them together. Edward Gibbon, in *The Decline and Fall of the Roman Empire*, states:

> In the end, more than they wanted freedom they wanted security. They wanted a comfortable life and they lost it all — security, comfort, and freedom. When the Athenians finally wanted not to give to society, but for society to give to them, when the freedom they wished for most was the freedom from responsibility, then Athens ceased to be free.

What about America today? Does it have the vigor, creative drive, and inner discipline to deal effectively with tomorrow's major concerns? Some of the major issues are the new wave of technology sweeping the world, shocking changes in American and worldwide financial markets, movement from large corporations to small businesses, having to compete in a global marketplace, a revolution currently underway in the delivery of financial services, the impact of government deregulation on the telecommunications system, churning change in transportation (particularly airlines), the instability of OPEC and the pain of lower oil prices for the economies of Texas, Oklahoma, and Louisiana, political debates over establishing ground rules for creating life through genetic research and development, and ethical questions in government, medicine, and television evangelism.

Don't forget the enormous influence of hi-tech medicine on health. Fluctuations in currency values are playing havoc on jobs and prices, creating tensions between world powers because of their stake in these changes measured in terms of jobs, unemployment, economic growth, and political stability. Changing demographics, moving from the baby boom generation to the baby bust era, will determine who is available to work and will dramatically alter demands for goods and services. And what about the enormously frightening issues surrounding AIDS?

Because there has been a gale-force rate of technological change just in the past few years, the existing tools of understanding and investments in machines, systems, computers, information, and know-how are often outdated even before workplace America can fully grasp their potential or put them to productive use.

The decade of the 1990's will be a constant foot race between science, technology, innovation, ethical questions, and world competition with the ever-present threat of obsolescence and uncertainty. Actions dealing with these issues have become high-risk decisions with high-stakes implications. There will be new winners and losers at government, business, and personal levels. Technical, economic, and cultural reasons for workplace problems are overwhelming and will overwhelm more and more organizations and individuals. Is it any wonder, in a fast-paced and high-stress workplace, that people, like machines, get caught up in the turmoil, become outdated, wear out, and end up being tossed aside?

PREPARATION AND MOTIVATION

Many people will be totally unprepared for the speed or magnitude with which technological breakthroughs occur before the turn of the century. Most reasons for this shortcoming are at the individual level — the inability to recognize signs forewarning new directions, the unwillingness to seek meaning or interpret implications of changes, and lack of motivation to deal with threats to economic security and personal well-being.

Intellectually lazy, people do not read available materials, seek information, or ask questions. They refuse to make the effort required to stay informed or to understand what they hear and see. Out of touch, they deny reality, bury their heads, and generally suffer as a consequence.

DIFFERENCE BETWEEN WINNERS AND LOSERS

Here is the bad news: Those who are paralyzed by routines of the past—using time-worn, traditional methods, doing what is comfortable, afraid to try anything new, believing they are immune to change —face disappointment and failure during working years and retirement. They will be counted among the weak. They are *the losers.*

But there is good news, too. Career success rests in the hearts and hands of those who seek opportunities, seize momentum, sense threats, and then deal with them through creativity and ingenuity. The greatest achievements will come to those who have the desire to excel, possess the skills to deliver, take the courageous actions necessary to break with tradition, and step out of the crowd.

Their opportunities for success will come by thumbing their noses at both peers and mediocrity. With a positive, winning, fresh-start, no-nonsense, inquisitive attitude, they maintain control in the face of un-certainty and ambiguity. They unshackle restraints and take charge of their destiny. They will be listed among the strong. They are *the winners.*

TRAITS OF WINNERS

Winners have six characteristics important to career survival and growth:

1. They stay ahead of others by seeking the forefront and the leading edge of change. Winners have vision.

2. They stay informed about impending change. Winners have curiosity.

3. They sense the need to change. Winners have flexibility.

4. They face change. Winners have courage of conviction.

5. They know when to respond to change. Winners have a feel for timing!

6. They do something about change —they have ability, motivation, and stamina! Winners take action!

Winners also have these qualities: They focus on opportunity, they pay attention to preparation, they understand self-discipline, and they apply self-management. Winners know who they are, what they believe, and for what they stand. They have self-determination and are willing to make self-sacrifice. They are positive and upbeat. They thrive on self-confidence and seek deep fulfillment. In control of their own careers and destiny at all times, winners know their source of inner strength.

They are willing to take risks to protect what they have and to promote their future. They work at managing change and make it a top priority in their lives.

WHO ARE THE LOSERS?

Losers are weak and faint-hearted. They grieve change. They mourn the passing of the present. Their hope is in the return of the past. They view life through a rear-view mirror. Losers desire opportunity without sacrifice. They insist on benefits without sweat and toil. They are unwilling to work hard or experience discomfort, and they thrive on self-pity. They suffer from self-paralysis. They offer excuses, complain, and blame others. They are negative and downtrodden. They are stagnant. Under duress, losers start to wilt and begin to die.

Their reward will be self-obsolescence. Their wounds are mostly self-inflicted. Their walk is stooped, and their eyes are often glazed and clouded with despair. This part of our human nature is sad, unnecessary, but predictable. Roman writer Juvenal said it best: "Luxury is more ruthless than war." History repeats itself.

There are two options. Decide now whether to be counted among the winners or listed among the losers in the career competition of the 1990's. My hope is that the tomorrows of everyone who reads my words will be exciting milestones of personal development. Do not let tomorrow be full of millstones of frustration, defeat, and disappointment.

CAREER FUTURE CHECKLIST

- Watch for important trends in your organization or industry.
- Keep ahead of change. Glean all current materials — newspapers, general magazines, and trade publications.
- Continue to learn. Attend professional meetings and developmental seminars.
- Listen to people talk. More importantly, hear what they have to say. Digest it. Decide what it means for you.
- Take action. If necessary, break old habits and routines. Shake loose from peers.
- Step into the future.
- Do it now.

PART II

STAYING IN CONTROL

ALL THE WAY

"Destiny is not a matter of chance — it is a matter of choice."

— William Jennings Bryan

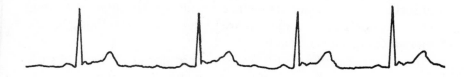

5

ARE YOU WHERE
YOU WANT TO BE IN LIFE?

*If you're not where you want to be in your career, go some-
where else, and do it now. It won't get any better. If you are where
you had rather be but can't stay there, move on quickly. Don't
look back.*

Who is in charge of your career? Coming to grips with this blunt question is the secret to whether you are on track in career. Are you fully
utilizing your skills and talents? Are you reaching the potential within
you? The answers start with you. With respect to personal career
management, there are three stages of emotional maturity.

First-stage maturity is best defined as breaking away from the
clutches of others, such as peers or well-meaning parents, and making
independent career decisions. It means being willing to take a risk and
stand on your own, sink or swim.

Second-stage maturity comes later in life, probably occurring
during the late thirties or forties, and is tied to the issues of mid-life. The
realization sets in: "My life is half over. Is there something I've missed?
There has to be more to life than what I've experienced so far." This is
the threshold of life's greatest challenge.

Second-stage maturity brings the strength to come to grips
seriously with your fundamental strengths and weaknesses as a person,
to concentrate on strong points rather than dwelling on shortcomings.
Second-stage maturity recognizes life as more than a physiological ex-

perience and begins to tackle seriously, on a spiritual level, the issues of career success versus personal satisfaction and inner fulfillment. Career goals begin to come into perspective with ethical values and basic beliefs as a human being. Are they in tune?

Third-stage maturity has to do with your response to adversity, such as being terminated from a job or becoming a casualty in the restructuring of corporate America. Situations may range from legitimate layoffs to being the target of personality conflicts, to office politics, to personal vendettas, to the shock of being fired for incompetence or other legitimate failures of your own doing.

Third-stage maturity means giving up real or imagined stability and security, overcoming the reality of losing control, coping with uncertainty, loneliness, embarrassment, and disappointment, handling defeat by putting it in the past, and casting about in unfamiliar terrain in search of tomorrow's employment.

Being unemployed, whatever the cause, comes as a devastating blow to self-esteem. But due to an unstable economy, these sudden job-loss situations are occurring with increasing frequency. To prepare for it, acknowledge the possibility of career shock and then take steps to protect your personal economic foundation and bolster your level of self-confidence.

Having third-stage maturity means being able to handle the challenges and pressures of moving from your present situation to where you must go to get your life back in balance and headed in the right direction. The acid test comes in being able to deal with sudden job loss and carrying out career change responsibilities while you stay in control.

FIND YOURSELF

The first seven profiles that follow are of frustrated people I know, know about, or believe to exist. They all have one thing in common: They are not where they want to be in their careers. Each person would rather be someplace else. All seven examples of career frustration relate to maturity stages one and two.

The last four profiles represent people who are comfortable in their jobs, and settled in their careers. They are really where they want to be, but have to go someplace else because of unavoidable circumstances. They have no choice. The one thing these four people have in common is that they lost their jobs and didn't see it coming. They were unprepared to face third-stage maturity. Can you identify with any of these eleven miserable people?

I WANT TO BE ELSEWHERE!

Bob

Being a successful attorney runs in Bob's family. Tradition dictated that Bob follow his dad and grandfather to law school. For the past eight years, Bob's life has been devoted to warranty deeds, contracts, and depositions. Why does Bob dislike his work? His buddy Tom is an investment broker in the East. Bob wishes he were, too.

Mary

Mary's mother, Becky, has been divorced for as long as Mary can remember. Life was tough at first, but Becky got her real estate license and did well. She insisted that Mary go to engineering school. Mary was excellent at math and scored high on all the entrance tests. Mary graduated with honors five years ago and had her pick of jobs. She remembered her mother's hopes and dreams for her, as well as who paid for her education. She wanted to make her mother happy. But now Mary is unhappy. She sits at a drafting desk all day long, dreaming about being an interior decorator.

Joe

For three generations, Joe's family has owned a building supply firm. Joe is attending business school at the state university. After graduation next year, he will go back home and groom to take over the family business. The only problem is that Joe really wanted to go to the Air Force Academy. Joe's dream was to become an astronaut.

Fred

A corporate executive for more than 20 years, Fred's title has a fancy ring to it. He makes major policy decisions. People are impressed. Fred eats at the luncheon club and travels in the best circles. There is a voice inside Fred telling him that what he does is meaningless. The voice of restlessness is getting louder. He is beginning to feel trapped. Somehow, attending cocktail parties, squeezing more performance out of operating divisions, raising funds for the charity, and viewing life from the 46th floor doesn't seem as appealing as it once did. Fred feels unproductive in his work and hollow inside as a person. Fred doesn't know what is happening to him or why. He only knows the pressure to get away from his present career circumstances of restlessness and unfulfillment is building.

Jason

Holding the position of columnist for a major business news service made Jason a powerful person. He had his finger on the pulse of the financial district. Jason's network of sources kept him on top of the issues. A favorable mention in his column was worth its weight in gold. Jason was the toast of the town. Everyone wanted to wine and dine him. He spent considerable time picking and choosing the invitations he would accept. But time caught up with Jason and he had to retire last year. His phone stopped ringing immediately. Jason learned the hard way. Throughout his career, he took himself and his position too seriously. Jason thought he was important. He also thought he had lots of friends. What Jason didn't understand was that he had no friends, only business contacts who were actually giving him the business. Jason's life passed him by. Now after 30 years in the limelight, Jason drinks alone.

Ann

Life was especially tough for Ann's father, an uneducated black man. Ann's dad got his start during the Depression as a dishwasher. After being discharged from the service, he settled in the Mid-west and took night school courses to sharpen technical skills learned in the Army. He became a maintenance man and was a good one. He could fix almost anything. Dad wanted Ann to have a career with dignity, so he insisted that she go to nursing school. Ann was a caring person. She was proud of her dad and respected his wishes. More than anything, she didn't want to hurt his feelings. For 12 years Ann has been a surgical nurse for a highly successful cardiovascular team. The doctors think she is the best and tell her so often. For the first few years Ann enjoyed her responsibilities in the operating room. She thrived on the pressure. But three years ago the magic wore off. She began to recognize the signs of burnout. Now Ann hates every day of it. She has discovered a new calling, working with handicapped children. This new career will require that she go back to school to be certified. Ann has saved thousands of dollars to finance her education. But last year, her mother died. Ann is the only child. Now Ann's dad calls her frequently, telling her how proud he is of his only daughter and the important work of being a nurse.

George

Recently promoted to assistant branch manager for the bank, George now sits behind the desk in his pinstriped suit. He makes loans, smiles at his customers, and makes sure the automatic teller machine stays in good working order. George learned to be a roofer when he was going through college. He was good at it. After graduation, George decided he was going to make something out of himself. He wanted to pursue a career of dignity and respect. Atlanta was a good place to be. Now as George processes loan applications, approves checks, and makes new business calls, he has an emptiness inside. He asks himself two good questions: "Outside my family, how many people know I'm here?" "How many people care?" He already knows the answer to both. Few and none! George really wants to go back home and enter the roofing business — to be his own boss — but he sees family circumstances as a barrier. Because of indecision, the door of opportunity to independence and liberation for George is probably closed forever. Someday he will probably be a branch manager.

R.I.P.
Here lies
Alice Jenkins
Born 1938
Died 1998
Existed 60 Years

DON'T BE AN ALICE JENKINS

What is the common denominator for all seven of these unfortunate souls? Each person wanted to be somewhere else. But they were either dominated by well-meaning parents, influenced by pressure from peers, or hamstrung by seemingly insurmountable barriers — real or imagined. What was the key to their dilemma? They depended on other people to get them to a career destination rather than by taking charge themselves. They were either unwilling or unable to make changes necessary to steer themselves toward greater inner fulfillment and personal satisfaction.

What will they do? For most, the answer is probably nothing. Feeling locked in, and without the courage of stage-one or stage-two maturity, they will wind up like all the countless thousands of Alice Jenkinses who wander through life nameless, faceless, with no goals, no drive, no commitment — just existing throughout a 40 year career.

Could you ever be one of these? Keep in mind that if you genuinely feel that your job is meaningless, boring, or largely without purpose it will not get any better, only worse. You can be assured there is little relief in sight. The key to resolving this dilemma is in answering these questions: *Where do I go from here? What does the future hold? What can be done about present circumstances? Who are the dominant influences in my life? Do they have a stake in my personal career success and happiness? Am I absolutely sure? Are they providing good information? What are the right answers to help me make good decisions? Do I even know the right questions?*

LEAVING WHERE YOU WANT TO BE

More and more people are suddenly finding themselves without the luxury of making their own career choices. The decision to move on to another job has been made for them. Their only considerations are: What to do now? Where to go from here? How to get there? Consider these four stage-three maturity profiles.

Melissa

The good news of acceptance in the company's management training program was exciting to Melissa. After 18 months in the classroom, learning computer technology and software applications, she was put into the field as a junior sales representative. Following two years of successful results calling on customers, she was offered a transfer to the Northeast to gain more experience with larger accounts. While it was a long way from Dallas, she accepted the opportunity and continued her progress as an exceptional employee. The promotion to marketing manager for the personal computer products division, coming three weeks before her 30th birthday, was really no surprise. She was surprised six months later, however, when she was terminated as part of the corporation's cost-reduction program. Melissa made one big mistake. She paid little attention to the company's year-end announcement that profits were off for the seventh consecutive quarter due to rising expenses, shrinking margins, and increased competition. The CEO warned then that tough decisions had to be made. She assumed since her performance was so good that rumored cuts in staff would not reach her. Melissa learned the hard way that you can't assume anything. No one is immune from the budget ax. Looking back, she realizes that she should have saved some money in a rainy day fund. She asks two questions: How will I make my monthly payments? How can I get back to Dallas where I belong?

Ed

As plant manager for the energy controls division, Ed followed performance goals to the letter. He made output and productivity quotas every year. He was a trouble shooter and was gifted with jack-of-all-trades skills. He felt indispensable to the company. In fact, annual performance appraisals reinforced Ed's high opinion of himself. When the company was merged, Ed was assured that his job was important and was urged to keep up the good work. Ed's boss called one day with the news that a new corporate controller had been sent in from Milwaukee to review the division's operating ratios. Three months later, when Ed's boss was terminated, Ed was advised that he should not be concerned. After acquisitions happen, he was told, top jobs are sometimes consolidated as an efficiency measure. What he was not told was that his division had been targeted to be spun-off to help pay for the "leveraged buyout." Ed joined the growing ranks of unemployed plant managers six months later. The Chicago outplacment firm gave Ed more bad news. There are far more executives being turned out across the country than there are new openings, they said. When asked if he had any other interests or skills, Ed replied that he had been told by his boss for years that he was an excellent manager and had a job for as long as he wanted it. What Ed didn't figure was that his boss wouldn't be there to fulfill his promise. Now 53, with two kids in college, Ed has a problem.

Betty

Betty was an excellent secretary. She responded well to all new office technologies and quickly learned to use the word processor. An extremely dedicated employee, with 26 years of service, Betty always knew she would be with the company for her entire career. Being single, she depended solely on the job for her livelihood and the non-contributory pension at retirement for her later years. Since high school, her job had been her life. Betty kept her shoulder to the wheel. She didn't have time for civic activity or professional affiliations. Somewhat introverted, she kept to herself and her assignments. She was totally loyal to her employer and to her work. The corporate culture was strongly paternalistic. Betty felt very good about that. When it was announced that the product line was being dropped and Pittsburgh's entire administrative staff was being eliminated, Betty had nowhere to turn. Someone in the New York corporate human resources department suggested she go to her professional contacts and do a little networking. Betty had no idea what they were talking about. Unprepared emotionally, mentally, and financially, Betty was set adrift at age 44.

Greer

Greer had been with his employer nearly 10 years when it finally dawned on him that working for a family business had one serious drawback that could not be overcome. When the chips were down, whatever the controversy, family members generally united against non-family employees. Greer was in charge of marketing. He stayed under constant pressure to increase sales revenues in a highly competitive market. The problem was that he couldn't deliver at the unit volume his boss demanded; not because he didn't try but because the production manager couldn't provide sufficient quantity of products on time and at an acceptable quality level. The boss called Greer in one day and chewed him out. When Greer explained the facts, his superior saw red. Greer had the guts to point his finger at the real problem. Unfortunately, the production manager was the boss' son and heir-apparent. Greer learned the hard way that in a family business blood runs thicker than water. In the case of a tie, the non-family member loses.

Do you think you might someday be in the shoes of Melissa, Ed, Betty, or Greer? Their sad predicaments occur with increasing frequency in America.

CAREER DIRECTION CHECKLIST

- Be alert. Job loss generally happens with little advance warning. Or maybe the early warning signs and signals were actually there, but were ignored or denied.
- Look ahead. When job loss statistics become a personal catastrophe it is too late for the present. Full attention must be turned toward the future and what to do about getting there.
- Focus on priorities. Dealing with job change, professional growth, career upsets, self-esteem, the search for happiness, and pursuit of continued achievement in life become very real at this point.
- Stay on top of the issues. Know what to do next, where to turn, how to plan, how to identify sources of support, how to develop the inner strength to cope, and how to take charge.
- Assess yourself. Think about the three stages of emotional maturity and make a personal assessment. How do you measure against them?
- Make plans. Follow through. Avoid being one of these 11 sad profiles happening daily somewhere in America.

6

WHY A JOB CHANGE
MAY HAPPEN TO YOU

Thousands of unemployed middle managers and executives are having difficulty finding a new job with at least equal pay and perks. Declining industries in America will continue to phase out thousands of jobs at all levels each year for the foreseeable future. No job is immune from extinction, including yours.

As an employee, conventional wisdom has always told you: "Once in a career, you have a job for life." The secret was to start at the bottom, work hard, and work yourself up the ladder. When you peaked out, you rode it out until age 65. Employers valued loyalty and rewarded it. They were even tolerant of job burnout or skills-obsolescence for a few years until retirement. A generation ago that reasoning was true. Few people changed occupations. Anyone who changed jobs more than once or twice during a career was suspect. But the ballgame has changed dramatically.

The average U.S. job now lasts only from three to four years. As previously stated, most people can expect to hold from five to six different jobs in a lifetime. Incredible? Yes, even frightening for some, but true.

Watch out for the guilt trip caused by obsolete workplace rules or outdated conventional wisdom about changing jobs. Odds are overwhelming that no one is likely to work for the same organization for 30 years, so don't plan on it. Why not? The answer is simple: Everyone is expendable. You may quit, be laid off, or be fired outright. Here are 36 reasons why.

20 REASONS WHY YOU MAY QUIT

1. The job doesn't deliver the promises made at time of employment. There is a wide gap between expectations and reality. You are betrayed by false promises and unrealistic expectations.

2. Incompetence! You are incompetent because of poor work habits or skills-obsolescence and are smart enough to leave before you are fired.

3. You are working for a bunch of losers. You subscribe to the principle that you can't soar like an eagle when surrounded by a bunch of turkeys.

4. There is no future. The job is a dead end. You are bored and experiencing burnout!

5. You are unwilling to accept a transfer to another department or location.

6. Unrealistic aspirations and dissatisfaction with slow progress leaves little hope for improvement.

7. The job doesn't financially support your lifestyle.

8. There is a change in personal life — marriage, pregnancy, spouse transfer, health problems.

9. Personal skills and job requirements are mismatched. You want to lead *people* but the job demands you manage *things*, or vice- versa.

10. Location — either you move or your employer moves. The cost of commuting or time required to travel back and forth is more than you can handle.

11. Recruitment to better opportunity.

12. You are a victim of sexual harrassment or of a failed office romance.

13. The company is going nowhere and you want to go someplace else.

14. Threats of merger, consolidation, acquisition, or restructuring create too much uncertainty. You seek more job security and stability.

15. You have the desire to be an entrepreneur and seek independence from the corporate straight jacket.

16. Career advancement dictates you need to move on. There is nothing against where you work — you just need to initiate the next step in your strategic plan toward job fulfillment and personal achievement.

17. You came to grips with a fundamentally bad decision — Dad wanted you to be a banker, but you wanted to be in computers. You tried it his way. Now you want to try it your way.

18. The grass looks greener across the fence. You are restless and have nomadic tendencies. You can't stay put.

19. Mid-life crisis sets in. You're on a new journey in life, and your present job isn't the final destination.

20. Last but not least is the "Young Turk vs. Old Jerk" or "Young Jerk vs. Old Turk" conflict between boss and subordinate. Personality conflicts, inability to communicate, or different leadership styles pose the insurmountable barriers. This results in finger-pointing. Something has to give. Somebody has to go. Who is the "Turk" and who is the "Jerk" is a matter of perception.

16 REASONS WHY YOU MAY BE FIRED

1. Incompetence.

2. Competence that threatens those entrenched in the organization who ought to be fired — but who are in control.

3. The entire profit center is a loser for reasons beyond your control. The division can't be salvaged.

4. You are caught in the first-to-go profitability crunch. Your specific job is expendable.

5. Merger or consolidation.

6. The boss loses a power struggle, and you are a casualty in the housecleaning.

7. Bad chemistry — you just don't fit the corporate culture. You have neither the "killer" instinct nor the "yes man" mentality.

8. Personal skills-obsolescence. You have gotten woefully behind with your job skills. You are a loser in the competition for available positions.

9. You are caught in a brutal numbers game — 50 were recruited to the company training program. Only 20 will make it and you are number 21.

10. You blow your cover! Your career plan doesn't include your present employer, but you didn't keep it concealed. You are considered to be disloyal by whomever you are supposed to be loyal to.

11. You don't play the office sex and favors game. You are now out of favor.

12. You do play the office sex and favors game and are doomed to an early exit as a result. Either way you lose.

13. Your employer discovers that you are experimenting with drugs or are too deep into the bottle.

14. A productivity and efficiency consultant is hired and discovers you.

15. The new trend is to eliminate layers of management. You just got eliminated.

16. All other reasons I haven't listed might be ready to happen to you. Write me if it happens.

IS IT TIME FOR A CHANGE?

Think clearly and objectively for a moment. Maybe forces outside your control are beginning to move against you at work. Perhaps there are some forces working over which you have no control. Or maybe something is going on deep inside of you, and the message from within tells you it's time for a change. If any of these circumstances are happening, then time is right to take charge and do something constructive to advance to the next career stage.

As you prepare to move on, take a serious reading of the circumstances. How much of the problem is really due to you? Remember, to the extent you are at fault, you must correct these weaknesses before they hurt you again. Don't ignore them. Other employers will see them, too. After the fact is always too late. Don't let a pattern of poor work habits develop. You will limp along until you deal forthrightly with any problems undermining your ability to hold a job or to grow in your career.

READING THE WARNING SIGNALS

There are several negative signals from within the organization that indicate it's time to go. Here are 19 to think about.

1. Important decisions become public knowledge or are well known within the company grapevine before you get the word.

2. Fellow workers turn on you as the topic of idle conversation. You become the subject of gossip by the water cooler or office copier crowd.

3. You don't get a promotion or better assignment. More importantly, the reason for being passed over is phony.

4. Your last salary increase doesn't fit past patterns of reward. The justification for the lower percentage doesn't make sense.

5. Your performance evaluation doesn't ring true. Your boss looks at the floor or out the window more than usual. Uncharacteristically, he or she fidgets while talking.

6. You have topped out in salary, job classification, or seniority. You feel stale. You are bypassed for younger people. You know the pattern.

7. Your organization changes strategies or priorities. You can't accept the shifts in thinking. You have become uncooperative and perhaps argumentative. You don't have the same commitment. You are no longer seen as a team player.

8. You don't get asked to lunch by your associates as much.

9. You are not called on or listened to in meetings any more.

10. You are not reappointed to a key committee.

11. You must represent the boss at a growing number of perfunctory civic functions, meaning your time is now less valuable to the business.

12. Your job changes dramatically causing you to spend your time on projects and activities for which you are ill-suited or in which you have little interest. This information is in previous performance evaluations. You are being snookered.

13. Assignments are being shifted to others with less seniority. Your job content weakens. You simply have little to do anymore. It's not by accident.

14. Your organization is about to be merged. Your department will be consolidated. If your job is in public relations, personnel, research,

or strategic planning, you are especially redundant and a prime candidate for the pink slip.

15. There is a lot of internal job movement. Bumping. Demoting. You are vulnerable due to low seniority.

16. You are in a declining, obsolete industry. The company is in a no-growth situation and suffers from financial doldrums. Stagnation sets in.

17. A "hot-shot" entrepreneurial manager is hired to breathe new life in the organization. He wants to bring in a new team and you know you're not on it.

18. You receive frequent calls from higher management with questions that put you on the defensive. A feeling of vulnerability develops.

19. You just know something is wrong, but you can't put your finger on it. Your instincts are talking to you. You can feel it in your bones.

MAINTAIN A STATE OF READINESS

For any of these reasons, you must stay ready to move. But to stay in control, you must have a competitive advantage. You must be marketable in terms of necessary skills and have something competitive to offer employers.

You must also have the ability to sell youself to close the deal. This might be the toughest hurdle to overcome. That's why you need to do some planning. Don't delay and have to scramble at the last minute. One of these days you might be cut loose from your job. Whatever the odds, it is far better to be safe now than to be sorry later. Be able to move on your own terms. To the extent possible, choose your own career timetable and operate at your own convenience.

My message is: Please don't let your career happen to you on somebody else's terms and to their advantage. Be the master of your destiny.

JOB READINESS CHECKLIST

- Stay alert. The key is in preparation and timing.
- Make contacts and develop a network.
- Have options and maintain flexibility.
- Be confident about your abilities and skills.
- Be courageous. Don't be paralyzed by fear of letting go or be concerned about unknowns of a new job and different surroundings.
- Maintain freedom. Don't be locked in and dependent on others.
- Focus on your strength.
- Maximize your potential.
- Be in a state of readiness.

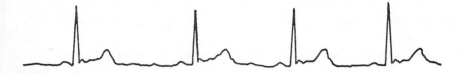

7

STRATEGIC PLANNING
FOR STRATEGIC GROWTH

Too many people's careers are dictated by the actions of others rather than by one's own plans. It shouldn't work this way. The secret is to establish your own plan and take charge of your own future.

When you, as an employee, primarily depend on others —bosses, supervisors, and peers — for career growth and job fulfillment, you may or may not get what you think you deserve. If you depend on yourself, however, you are more likely to be alert and to make positive things happen, although not necessarily easily and conveniently. Positioning yourself is the key. Concentrate on mobility, flexibility, networking, regrouping, retraining, and on rethinking the future. The focus of your efforts must always be on your SELF! On you. Never forget this!

TEN SIMPLE TRUTHS YOU NEED TO FACE

1. Few of your fellow workers are ever in a position to ensure job stability for you or even for themselves. Even fewer will be in a position to look after your job security when the chips are down. Practically no one will be able to go to the mat for you at a time of job crisis. Why?

2. Due to dramatic changes in business ownership, leadership from the top downward is turning over. Businesses are tightening up.

Thousands of companies are being reorganized, consolidated, or stripped down. As a result, corporate cultures, chemistries, and payrolls are also going through severe adjustment. It's a transition that shakes every level.

3. Demands for better productivity and increased profits are causing companies to look hard at wage and salary expense. The ground rules for hiring, compensating, and retaining people are changing. Uncertainty and confusion reign.

4. People who, in the past, could help you are heading for the trenches themselves. They are being shifted, promoted, demoted, transferred, retired, fired, or are quitting in disgust and frustration.

5. Many who aren't facing the ax are feeling nervous anyway and are likely looking for a job themselves. Job meltdown is causing people to head for fallout shelters.

6. While your employer can promise anything, few people above you can guarantee delivery further out than six months and certainly not beyond a three-year personal strategic plan.

7. Under adverse conditions, senior executives generally make the major mistakes, but it's the middle managers and rank-and-file employees who get fired.

8. Among the real growth industries in America are:
- Outplacement firms
- Employee assistance programs
- Career planning services
- Employment agencies
- Drug/alcohol treatment centers
- Marriage counselors and divorce courts
- For-profit psychiatric hospitals

9. The new losers are firms supplying 30-year service pins and catering retirement parties.

10. Best-selling business and "how-to" books consistently deal with self-analysis, resumé preparation, job-hunting, and other career employment topics.

In short, making a job or career change is okay. As pointed out earlier, you will initiate some of the changes. Some will be inflicted upon you. But you must be prepared for either situation. Always expect the best, but prepare for the worst. To get going, you need a road map, a specific, well-thought-out strategic plan. There is an old saying: *"If you don't know where you are going, any road will get you there."* That's why you need a compass for guidance. Reach your destination on purpose by design — not by accident. All you have working for you is your ability and time. Don't waste either. You need a plan.

THE 75 PERCENT RULE

If you get nothing else out of this book, remember the 75 percent rule of life: 75 percent of everything good that happens to you happens because of what you do *for* yourself. And 75 percent of everything bad that happens to you happens because of what you do *to* yourself. Most wounds are self-inflicted due to poor planning, faulty timing, bad action, or inaction.

DOING FOR YOURSELF: THE SELF-FACTORS

There are positive self-factors and negative self-factors competing to influence your actions and attitudes. It is important to understand this and to be guided by positive self- factors. Here are twenty-one positive self-factors to consider. Some have already been mentioned in previous chapters. Select the ones that apply to you and focus on them to stay on track in achieving your goals. This is the 75 percent rule in action.

Positive Self-Factors

Self-Reliance	Self-Restraint	Self-Worth
Self-Preservation	Self-Fulfillment	Self-Esteem
Self-Promotion	Self-Initiative	Self-Dignity
Self-Management	Self-Starting	Self-Discipline
Self-Survival	Self-Refreshed	Self-Examination
Self-Awareness	Self-Motivated	Self-Sacrifice
Self-Development	Self-Assessment	Self-Confidence

NEGATIVE SELF-FACTORS

On the other hand, negative self-factors become self-inflictions that drag you down. While there are other negative self-factors, here are twelve to deal with. Study each one carefully. Be honest. Do any sound like you? Do everything possible to minimize their impact.

Negative Self-Factors

Self-Centered	Self-Defeating	Self-Pity
Self-Cynical	Self-Destructive	Self-Importance
Self-Demise	Self-Paralysis	Self-Satisfying
Self-Doubt	Self-Delusions	Self-Condemnation

WHY SET GOALS?

Goals give direction and purpose. Florence Chadwick, the great long distance swimmer, who swam the English Channel many times, once tackled the 20-mile distance from Catalina Island to the California coast.

It was a cold day, currents were very rough, the water was chilled and visibility was virtually zero due to dense fog. Boats on both sides of Chadwick bore men who fired guns into the water to scare off sharks.

Only one-half mile from her goal Chadwick gave up. Later, when asked why she quit so close to her destination, she replied that it was not the currents, it was not the chill, it was not the sharks. It was the fog. Chadwick said she simply could not see her goal and became discouraged.

The same is true for each of us as career planners. Uncertainty, a lack of purpose, and no sense of direction can keep us in a fog and cause severe loss of desire and motivation. We must always have a vision which offers clear, crisp objectives. We must stay in control. We must heed the signs of change around us.

Setting attainable career and personal goals increases the likelihood of positive self-factors being the dominant influence in your life. Goals will offset any negatives that occur because of a lack of purpose and direction.

Setting goals helps force you to come to grips with accepting full responsibility for yourself and for others who depend on you. Finally, setting goals helps open up fresh ideas and new directions. In fact, the goal setting process is exciting, not unlike plunging into the exhilarating waters of a cool mountain lake. You feel vibrant and alive as you keep all senses attuned to the environment. But setting goals is easy. Sticking to them is the hard part.

HOW OLD ARE YOU?

Here is a practical reason for taking charge and charting your own course. First, answer this question: How old are you? 25? 35? 45? 55? Find your age in this Life Expectancy Table, showing how long you can expect to live, depending on health and lifestyle, and barring misfortune.

LIFE EXPECTANCY TABLE*		
(National Center for Health Statistics)		
If you are:	Life Expectancy:	
Age	*Male*	*Female*
25-29	73	80
30-34	73	80
35-39	74	80
40-44	74	80
45-49	75	80
50-54	75	81
55-59	76	82
60-64	78	83

*These life expectancy projections have been increasing slightly each year due to improved health care technology, heightened awareness of the need for physical fitness, and proper eating habits. Unchecked spread of the AIDS virus could alter the death rate.

Let's say you are 35. Statistically, if you are a male, you have near-ly 40 years in front of you. A female has 45 years. That's a long time.

WHAT IS YOUR MISSION AND PURPOSE?

Make specific plans and have clearcut objectives about how to use the productive career years ahead for your benefit. First, establish a mission in life.

How important are family, money, achievement, prestige, travel, geography, and friends? An assessment of these basic values and personal priorities will help determine an appropriate career plan and help find the right job. Since you will spend most of your waking hours at work, make absolutely sure you enjoy them. Make your job work for you. You must determine the best niche in the workplace based on your abilities and goals.

Keep in mind that the journey through the ages and stages of life and career will be on a curvy, bumpy road. Job factors and personal considerations important now will most likely change, maybe even several times. There will be plenty of surprises along the way. But that's to be expected in a nomadic, unpredictable world. All the rules that emphasize career-long job stability and 30-year retirement celebrations have been tossed out the window.

Always focus on self-management and self-survival to eliminate the chance of self-pity and self-destruction later. You are all you have, and 40-45 years is a very long time. You owe it to yourself to demand a full measure of life. But living with meaning requires that you manage yourself wisely. Just remember, you have to earn your keep and it's up to you to make life happen *for* you all the way.

BE AWARE OF TWO CORPORATE EVILS

1. Corporate Seduction

Employment managers are paid to woo workers with talk about future promises: job opportunities, career paths, growth potential, fringe benefits, and retirement plans. Cut through all the cosmetic conversation with straight talk about immediate job issues important to you.

Negotiate the deal on the front end in writing. Know all the ground rules at the beginning. Pay little attention to anything said about pensions or long-term benefits. Ignore any "carrots" dangled out to be harvested beyond three years. Obtain a clear understanding of immediate training programs and professional development opportunities. If unclear, try to determine your likely placement within the organization after orientation. Ask questions. You have a right to know.

The point is this: If everything essential isn't nailed down at the beginning, you will get nailed in the end. In today's uncertain world of mergers, consolidations, and cutbacks, chances are the ground rules will be different in three to five years. Don't depend on long-term promises. The future will take care of itself only if you do the right things from the beginning. This is working smart. If you don't take care of yourself, nobody else will. Count on it.

2. Corporate Voodoo

Most organizations have a medicine man whose prime function is to incite the natives with drum-beating talk about loyalty and motivation. The CEO, department head, plant manager, your supervisor, or all the above may take the role. Corporate propaganda says that employees belong to some kind of closely knit company family. Be wary of it. Make absolutely sure that loyalty is a two-way street. Determine if your employer will be as loyal to you as is expected of you.

Ask this basic question: Can your employer really provide loyalty during uncertain times ahead? What is actually being delivered except pep talk? Look for evidence of the company's ability to deliver on promises made during the interviews and while on the job.

Loyalty is an intangible quality that must be redefined in today's terms. Loyalty meant much more in yesteryear when the odds were favorable you would remain with the same organization though a career. Employers could give solid assurances about the future. But in today's workplace, the definition of loyalty is diluted. Chances are the organization won't even remain intact. Will ownership always stay the same? Will current management always remain at the helm? Will your supervisor always be there in time of need? The answer to each is "No."

If a company demands loyalty, seek a specific definition of it and determine what will be given by management in return. Expecting and giving blind loyalty is naive, unreasonable, and short-sighted in today's fast changing world. Relying on it or giving it could be career suicide. Understand this fact of life and deal with it as you work your career plan.

WHAT DOES YOUR RESUMÉ SAY?

A critical point often overlooked in career planning is that a resumé and reputation are built by job performance day by day. Give your very best every day. While drawing your paycheck, always be positive. Keep a winning attitude about your employer. Let your job performance and attention to important duties speak for themselves. This is loyalty in action. But stay in charge. Never let your shield of self-reliance down in the process.

21 GUIDELINES FOR STAYING IN COMMAND

1. Remain razor sharp. Keep your eye out for opportunity. Always test career goals. Investigate all leads and possibilities based on qualifications, personal interests, and likelihood of achieving existing career goals where you are. Be objective and hard-nosed in developing answers to these questions. Be systematic in the process of finding, getting, and holding jobs that help you grow based on your ability and priorities at every career stage.

2. Don't engage in wishful thinking or fantasy goal setting. Take your career in specific stages. Map your career advancement three years at a time. Don't plan concretely beyond three years (see Appendix for more details on three-year planning reviews). Keep all available options open. Do not lock into the present.

3. Take nothing for granted. As has been stressed, do not asssume you will be with the same organization your entire career. Job change, not job stability, will become the standard. Don't be frustrated or intimidated by the desire or need to change jobs or careers. Take change in stride. This is a normal pattern of personal career management coming in the 1990's.

4. Whether you are a career beginner or are in mid-career, you cannot know whether a new job suits you until you are actually on it. There is no substitute for getting your feet wet, getting "hands-on" experience. If you like your job, great. If you don't, give it your best effort

for a reasonable period of time, perhaps a year or two. If you don't remain upbeat, determine what's happening and why. Try to fix it. Then, if you still don't like your job for reasons beyond your control, change. If the situation is beyond repair because of office politics or poor leadership, move out as quickly as possible. Never be miserable. Let me repeat, never be miserable, because the damage done to your inner psyche can often be devastating and take months, even years, to repair. Your mental and physical health could depend on how you deal with this matter.

5. There are several reasons why you might not like your job. You may find that you are under-employed. The job may not challenge your intellectual skills, your vocational interests, and your general aptitude. The job may turn out to be routine or just plain boring.

You may find that you are over-employed. If so, you have misread the situation in terms of job skills required and you are in over your head. Stop treading water. Don't wait around to be discharged because of your own incompetence.

The company may be a bad place to work for a lot of reasons you can only discover once there. Unfortunately, very few managers and supervisors really know how to develop trainees or to lead their people. If this is true in your situation, you will suffer as a consequence. Don't suffer indefinitely.

You may be victimized by poor leadership style from the top. Bad management from the executive suite oozes down through various layers of management, stifling creativity and enthusiasm all the way to the bottom. Don't be mired down in it.

You may discover that the place is simply poorly run at every level and can't be rehabilitated. Don't let bad leadership warp your enthusiasm and dampen your desire to grow professionally. Get away from this type of situation before you become targeted for a pink slip by being blamed for the organization's faulty performance.

6. One approach to staying in command is to size up the power structure. Define the corporate structure. Understand the ground rules and how decisions are really made. The CEO will very likely have a massive ego and a strong personality. In fact, over time, the business collectively will take on many of the same interpersonal characteristics of the boss. You will soon know whether you like the chemistry. If the CEO's management style has been in place for a while, more than likely your department head or immediate supervisor is a survivor. This may mean he or she is pretty much a product of the CEO's leadership style.

Depending on the existing culture, your immediate boss may have a weak personality and a Caspar Milquetoast approach to management. This pathetic style too often results from having been beaten down to the behavior required to survive under the CEO's reign.

7. With all the technological and economic changes taking place, leadership styles that focus on genuine employee participation and personal well-being have been temporarily outmoded. Most firms that have adopted Japanese management styles, "quality circles," or other faddish leadership approaches generally apply only lip service to the concepts. Most don't know how to implement these systems effectively. Downward pressure on profits and productivity will encourage this type of experimentation as insecure managers seek novel solutions to elusive problems. The result will be continued stress, uncertainty, and frustration. Don't let these influences take a toll on you.

8. Management textbooks describe many leadership models. When all is said and done, there are only two alternatives in the real world. Managers are either "me-oriented" or "you-oriented." If they are *you-oriented* then you will have a chance to learn and develop, to gain from the experience, to be a better person for the time you spend there. If the manager is *me-oriented*, you have little chance to grow. In this situation, do everything you can to be transferred or get out of the organization altogether.

9. Most of your troubles will be caused by personality deficiencies or leadership weaknesses of your supervisor. Too many people live with anger. Psychiatrist Ross Campbell confirms this when he writes about the nature of anger:

> You see immature ways of handling anger every day. You see an employee doing poor work to undermine the employer's interests. You see a principal abusing a teacher. You see a teacher subtly working against a principal. You see special interest groups attempting to hurt others materially. Immature handling of anger is on every hand. It is one of the greatest problems in business today, resulting in poor attitudes in employer and employee alike. Sixty to eighty percent of problems in any organization are personnel related, because too few people have learned how to deal with anger maturely.[2]

Remember, there are some people out there who are difficult to get along with. Motivated by their own personality deficiencies, they are arrogant, self-serving, pompous, dictatorial, difficult, and downright devious. They thrive on draining your enthusiasm and destroying your self-worth. If you find that your future depends on this type of person in any shape, form, or fashion, get away from him before he dampens your spirit and poisons your attitude.

10. Spend time in candid self-examination. Make sure you are giving your job a full measure of expertise and enthusiasm. Always meet your employer at least halfway. If you aren't, take the steps to understand why and correct the problem to the extent that it is within your control.

11. Avoid turf struggles. Stay away from office politics and office politicians. These are phony substitutes for achieving results. Gossip is poison. Avoid such purveyors of human misfortune.

12. Keep your personal "non-work" problems away from work. Nobody wants to hear your complaints and personal concerns. Remember the 80/20 rule of complaining. Eighty percent of those to whom you complain don't care, and the other twenty percent are glad you have the problem. So don't complain and don't associate with negative people. This practice can and usually will be detrimental to your job health.

13. Develop sustainable relationships with work associates. Do not let a negative person or superior warp your personality. A simple principle is to be helpful to others. Be as humble as possible. Work at making others feel important. Be able to give and to take. Accept criticism and give praise. Develop a sense of belonging. Try to feel at home. Always be the "real you." Get as comfortable with your job circumstances as you can, but always respect yourself. Understand that you deserve respect. Most importantly, you should always demand respect. Be careful to take advice only from those who support you and who will benefit from your success. Never compromise these underlying principles of self-worth.

14. Keep an eye on the obsolescence factor of your industry. Is it a growth industry or is it mature? Could it be aging? Is it on the decline? Are stock brokers recommending the stocks of key firms in your industry? If so, for what reasons? What are recent earning trends? Are top executives paying themselves excessive bonuses? Even more important, are good earnings, high dividends, and large bonuses a sign of excellent performance and real growth, or is the company actually deplet-

ing its capital? A better question to ask is: How much of the organzation's current earnings are being ploughed back as an investment for the future? This is a key indicator of the company's staying power and your long-term employment potential. Check various U.S. Department of Commerce publications and the Bureau of Labor Statistics for employment forecasts that have an impact on your industry. Translate the answers to your firm. Do not be lulled to sleep by past glory. Again, beware of corporate voodoo. Corporate success is short-term. Nothing is sacred. Do not stay on a sinking ship. Keep an eye on growth industries and make sure your skills are sharp and marketable to healthy organizations of the future. Don't be victimized by obsolescence shock.

15. Don't waste time if your job or organization isn't as it was represented. Don't be terrorized by bad "people management" — life is too short. If job circumstances and career interests conflict, be prepared to invoke the next step in your three-year strategic plan. Always seek alternatives and develop options. This will give you maximum flexibility to move on. There are far too many discontented people in today's workplace. More than half of America's work force suffers from job-related unhappiness at some level. Basically, all these people are caught in jobs which are unsatisfying, unchallenging, frustrating, threatening, and probably dead-end. This is a prime reason why stress, depression, chemical abuse, and suicide are significant killers in America. Don't be a statistic.

16. If you decide to look for another job, do it quickly and confidentially. *Do not* trust anybody where you work or confide in anyone within the organization. Job-hunting will be interpreted as an act of disloyalty and could lead to an earlier exit than you intended. The worst situation is to tip off management to your career plans and be terminated as a result.

17. Even if you are happy and content, begin now to develop an outside network of those who can keep you informed of job opportunities later on. Keep in touch with people who can help you professionally. Networking can be helpful in achieving success in a mobile, uncertain world. If you intend to be the master of your destiny, use the assistance of others in professional associations, trade groups, former schoolmates, civic involvements, and even competitors. You should have a specific game plan for organizing a job assistance network and for keeping it alive so you can call on it when necessary. But the key is

to develop and nurture contacts while you are still on the job. Don't wait until you quit to begin networking. It's best to do what you can for others while you can lead from strength. You will be in a better position to call in favors later on. Do not ever feel you are using people. Chances are, you are simply tapping an existing "workplace survival" network in which you are also being perceived as a potential source of assistance. It's all a part of today's "musical jobs" game.

18. Fully understand the true meaning of the following terms: *business associates, business relationships, business colleagues, business contacts,* and *business friends.* They are just that. The key word is *business.* When you go away, they go away. If they are inside your organization, they are as lasting as your tenure. If these contacts are in your industry, they will last as long as you are connected to the industry. There is nothing wrong with cultivating and having professional relationships, but recognize them for what they are. If you are lucky, maybe one in a thousand business acquaintances becomes a close friend. Why? The real reasons for the relationship are proximity and mutual dependency. You need one another to get the job done. When that need disappears, the relationship evaporates as well. Do not have your feelings hurt if the telephone stops ringing when you depart. Very likely, it will. Expect it. Don't be disappointed when it happens.

19. If you plan to leave your present place of employment, be sure to do some thoughtful career planning first. Don't panic and take the first thing that comes along. When you identify the right opportunity, be sure to nail everything down in writing before you give your notice.

20. If you decide to resign, do it very professionally, and with dignity. Go out with class and by the book. Be timely and put in writing only the bare essentials. Write in good taste and with style. Demonstrate no anger or bitterness. Do not get personal. Even offer to train your replacement. But be prepared: Even under pleasant circumstances, you may or may not get a favorable or sympathetic response to your resignation, but don't worry about it. Keep in mind that when you leave, your employer and former associates will likely shut the door behind you. Most people who leave their place of employment due to a resignation find that they are unwelcome if they return for a personal visit, so don't worry about going back. Chances are you didn't have any real friends there anyway. Under a worst case situation, you have unknowingly become the convenient scapegoat and have been saddled with all the problems they are experiencing.

21. At all costs, wherever you are in your career or whatever your present job circumstances, protect your self-worth and personal dignity. Never compromise these principles, either on your existing job or during a career change. These qualities reflect your basic beliefs and represent what you stand for at the very core of your existence. They are your most prized asset, representing your values at the most fundamental level.

SIZING UP WINNER AND LOSER COMPANIES

Some organizations, particularly those which are smaller, younger, and more entrepreneurial in spirit, reflect the leadership style and management philosophy required to respond to changes. They have the best opportunity to prosper in the 1990's. While still in the minority, some exist and more are emerging. They offer refreshing hope. Here are some of the characteristics of tomorrow's winners in corporate America. See how your employer stacks up.

THE WINNERS ...

1. ... know how and when to untie fortunes from technologies, styles, markets, products, and business methods that will become obsolete. They are not stuck like glue to the past or present.

2. ... have the right people in place to make successful and timely transitions to new products, new markets, and new thinking. They have the good sense of timing required to get positive marketplace responses.

3. ... don't overestimate their strength and don't underestimate their competition. They aren't cocky or arrogant.

4. ... don't take their customers or their own ability to provide services for granted. They run scared only as a matter of strategy.

5. ... understand that forces outside the firm's control dictate ultimate success. They have the ability to recognize and deal with external forces.

6. ... focus on external effectiveness, not just internal efficiency. They concentrate first on doing the right things, then on doing things right.

7. ... are not victimized or intimidated by conventional wisdom. They have the willingness to accept criticism for taking the steps necessary to compete before the reasons for taking those steps are obvious. Criticism may come from employees, board of directors, shareholders, stockbrokers, the financial media, public interest groups, unions, politicians, and peers.

8. ... do not cherish old traditions. They have willingness to change.

9. ... they encourage openness, innovation and creativity, freedom to question, and information sharing when it comes to the leadership of employees. They tolerate mistakes and offer support to employees.

10. ... have the confidence of their employees. They give trust and receive commitment.

11. ... reward long-range thinking, planning, and decisions, not just current year financial performance.

12. ... insist on intellectual honesty. Executive management tells the board of directors the truth, not just what they think the board wants to hear. Directors are independent-minded, active, inquisitive, and involved. They are interested in the long-term well-being of the company, not just in accepting fees and feeding egos.

13. ... do not believe their own public relations, press releases, annual reports, and other pronouncements for public consumption. They listen to what financial analysts have to say about their successes with grain of salt. They are not "big headed."

THE LOSERS ...

1. ... are asleep, bloated, inwardly-oriented, arrogant, autocratic, and ego-driven.

2. ... cling to old technologies, old leadership styles, old product lines, old accounting methods, old performance measures, old reward systems, old markets, and old attitudes among executives, managers, workers, and unions.

3. ... think they are invulnerable.

4. ... confuse "can do" with "can't fail." They assume that because they have won in the past they will win in the future, that superiority and victory are automatic.

5. ... see technology, research and development, and people as overhead, not as investments.

6. ... assume they already have answers to questions instead of seeking them.

7. ... allow executives' personal objectives to get in the way of the corporate job to be done.

8. ... grieve change, live in the past, and long for a return to the good old days! They have a "this too will pass" mentality.

9. ... become dependent on tradition and prior successes, misread trends and momentum, have no vision, are paralyzed and maybe even brain dead.

10. ... are making record profits and paying record dividends, but because they are not reinvesting in the organization's future, are actually milking the company for salaries and bonuses and are liquidating the business in the process.

11. ... are cosmetic in dealing with issues. They assume that they can handle new competition, new trends, new environments, and new ages with old ways, old cultures, with the same people in high places, the same approaches, and the same styles.

12. ... try to camouflage an outdated organization and to rationalize shortcomings by changing the corporate name to a "high-tech" sound while everything else negative remains the same.

13. ... don't try to understand that the further a company drifts from traditional sources of strength, the greater becomes its vulnerability to failure.

14. ... either don't think they have a problem or don't want to believe they have a problem.

15. ... have no courage of conviction. Management wants to know the truth that sets them free, not the truth that hurts, and without courage of conviction, employees contribute to this lie by telling management what it wants to hear.

These qualities hold true for profit and non-profit employers alike. Notice that the threads common to winners are vision, flexibility, a desire to change, a willingness to take risks, courage, openness, honesty, an orientation to people, and an appetite for information. They are firmly grounded in ethics about their purpose. Sprinkled throughout all these qualities is a will to win and a common sense approach. They get the job done, and their employees are part of the team.[3]

ONE LAST WORD ABOUT GOALS

As America moves forward during this period of dramatic workplace transition, you should move forward with it. Pay attention to your attitude. When all is said and done in dealing with change, people normally adopt one of two views of the world.

View One says that "the formula" works. View One assumes that past performances and achievements will be rewarded in the future. This view provides a broad comfort zone complete with order, routine, and predictability. Life is seen as a steady course. The prevailing attitude is *"nothing new is happening around here."* Everything is wonderful in a Garden of Eden mentality. The future is seen as an extension of the past.

While life goes on for those possessing this view, lessons are learned too late, if ever, and are soon forgotten. Their foundation slowly crumbles, and their strengths erode. Those who possess View One get caught and become losers in the battle of change. View One is the path to obsolescence, disappointment, and failure.

View Two, on the other hand, says simply that there are no guarantees. Anything can, and very likely will, happen throughout a career. Nothing is certain or predictable. Only change is inevitable. View Two is an entrepreneurial, high-adventure approach to a career, requiring ongoing preparation and patience. It's risky and has a very limited comfort zone, but perseverance and excellence are rewarded.

The choice of approaches to career and life in general is yours. One thing is certain: Your future will not be automatic. You have no guarantees, only the opportunity to rise to your potential. Robert Browning tells us *"Our aspirations become our possibilities."* Keep in mind the following: "If I want it to be, it's up to me."

STRATEGIC PLANNING CHECKLIST

- Depend on yourself, not others, to make positive things happen.
- Establish and maintain a mission in life.
- Choose your vocation based on your mission.
- Plan in three-year cycles.
- Beware of corporate voodoo and seduction.
- Give your best while in a job. Be positive.
- Be alert to trends in your organization and make decisions accordingly.

PART III

WORKING SMART

AT EVERY STAGE

Everyone lives on the edge of job obsolescence and the threshold of career opportunity .... You can't conduct your business or professional affairs in the future as you have in the past and be successful.

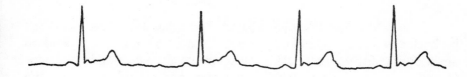

8

TOUGH DECISIONS FACING COLLEGE STUDENTS AND OTHER CAREER BEGINNERS

Are today's young people getting yesterday's advice about tomorrow's jobs?

Young people must become career-wise and job-smart early. Because the world is changing so fast, they must stay in touch with workplace realities or get lost in the shuffle.

Career management is a lonely business requiring much self- discipline. I've spent 30 years observing young people struggle, stumble and fall, then pick themselves up, get going, and grow to achieve success. The most important advice I can give you, the career beginner, is summarized in the following 15 checkpoints. My information is deceivingly simple. The rest of the chapter builds on these points and describes them in more detail.

GETTING CAREER BEARINGS

1. Accept full responsibility for every aspect of your career. Don't lay back and wait for somebody else to do something. Don't depend on anybody else for your success — not parents, family, friends, acquaintances, peers, or anybody else. Get going on your own initiative and take nothing for granted. Stay in control at all times.

2. At some point (and the sooner the better) every person must come to grips with the reality that no one else is looking after his or her career. Few people outside of family really even care. Every person must develop his or her own career momentum by taking charge at several levels: developing technical skills, vocational interests, and career planning; first-job seeking efforts; and coping with early career frustrations, disappointments, and surprises.

3. Get going in the right direction. This includes becoming aware early of your aptitudes and career interests. Don't let anyone else determine your career choice. Final determination of whether a job is best for you must be your decision. Seek advice and weigh it, but you must decide for yourself what is best.

More and more young people are learning tough lessons the hard way. After graduation, when employed in their first job, they discover they made a big mistake. They selected the wrong major field of study or choice of career to pursue. Overly influenced by parents, peers, family, friends, role models, or by their own perception of so-called "glamorous careers," too many young people choose the wrong college preparation or first job.

If this has happened to you, don't drift along hoping something good will happen. Do whatever is required to correct the mistake.

4. Be alert to new job trends and emerging occupational developments. The job market is extremely fluid and is subject to fast-breaking changes. Keep up with employment forecasts.

Look in the mirror. Do your abilities match skills currently in demand? What are the odds of finding work fitting your interest? Can you improve the odds for success by improving your skills or marketability?

5. Be honest with yourself. Make mature decisions. Take mature actions. Your objective should be to deliver the very best you have to offer an employer every day. From the first day on the job, be the real

you — not a copy of somebody else. Always lead from your strengths. This is the only way you can be sure you are giving your job a fair chance. This approach will help you assess from the outset whether your career is heading in a successful direction.

6. Most career beginners experience "reality shock" on their first job. Personal expectations and job realities often clash with unpleasant consequences. Because of this bad experience (and it happens with too much frequency) there is enormous turnover in the first jobs. Reality shock is predictable and not unusual, so don't worry too much if it happens. Just be sure you have done your part to minimize the discomfort. Understand your abilities, have realistic expectations, and don't be lured into jobs without doing your homework. Ask questions. Be satisfied for yourself on important issues before accepting.

7. Count on changing jobs at least five or six times during your career. This may happen due to a variety of circumstances: the job is misrepresented, you don't like your work, your superior doesn't like you, you don't fit in, you become expendable due to employee cutbacks, the organization folds, the business is sold or merged and there is no place for you, you move to a new geographic location, your personal needs or career interests change as you mature.

8. By necessity, both emotionally and economically, your career and work must become the center of your life if you are to have independence, social freedom, psychological stability, and financial flexibility. No work means no money, no freedoms, no growth, and no happiness. Do not take this point lightly.

9. Work that genuinely satisfies you will take care of most human needs. Be sure your job satisfaction and your motivation to work is more than just to make money in order to pursue other interests. A focus on money as work's primary reward is not mature, career-oriented thinking.

10. After college, a happy, fulfilling life is much more than having a good time, spending money, acquiring possessions, and getting ahead by material standards. Far too many young people seek these things early and discover later that life has been an empty experience. Why? They started at the wrong place with the wrong goals.

11. A career should be a growth process: intellectually, materially, and spiritually. For your career to be balanced and to move ahead on all fronts, hard choices have to be made. There are many trade-offs: pleasure versus work; skills improvement and professional development

versus time spent in recreation, travel, and loafing; spending versus saving; focusing efforts on today versus planning for the future; and balancing self-gratification needs with commitments to others.

12. Priorities for comprehensive self-management include: skills development, time utilization, stress-control and mental fitness, physical fitness, personal financial flexibility, and spiritual growth. Balancing these priorities is very important — stay aware of each of them.

13. Begin dealing now with the question of basic values and personal ethics to guide your actions in the work world. With the nation being hammered with revelation after revelation of unethical behavior in government, business, and church, you need to take a stand on the question of moral conduct. Do not be swayed by advertising, television shows, news coverage, actions of peers, or any other source that says: "Anything goes," "You only go around once," "Everybody is doing it," "Nice guys always finish last." This is nonsense! I repeat: nonsense!

Short-term self-interest based on humanism, greed, ambition, and selfishness is self-destructive. Undergird personal ambitions and job requirements with values reflecting honesty, empathy for others, kindness, patience, tolerance, fair dealing, and a sense of sharing. You can be ethical and get what you want, but it may be difficult to accomplish. You may have to look hard and may even have to make job changes or career moves to find it. But that's okay, because when all is said and done "the good guys" do finish first.

Demonstrate strong leadership and exhibit positive peer pressure in what you stand for. Let your actions speak. This approach might result in hard knocks now, but later on you will be glad you did.

14. At all costs, protect your self-worth and personal dignity. Pay whatever price is required to preserve your reputation. Don't take risks with your good name. Don't let personal habits and immature behavior be your undoing. Self-worth must be at the top of your priority list.

15. While going through life, you will become a slave to anything that defeats you. Do not let people or circumstances defeat you. Do not defeat yourself. Have a vision for yourself. Let it grow. Help it along. Do not let your vision perish.

ENTERING A FAST-CHANGE WORKPLACE

Uncertainty, instability, and change are the three constants in the world. The pace is rapid and volatile. Changes in employment opportunity, job content, and in the technical abilities needed for premium positions are coming faster than ever before. Getting, staying, and growing in a job is a new ball game.

New winners and new losers among professions, industries, companies, and individuals will surface during the 1990's. Some industries will die, while others will emerge. Throughout your lifetime you will live and work in the shadow of skills obsolescence. You will manage your personal life and professional career in an atmosphere of unpredictability. In the world of tomorrow, no one will be able to let up or give up and still keep up.

BE YOUR OWN BOSS

Leave absolutely nothing to chance. Do not depend on others to make things happen for you. If you do, the chances are good that things won't happen to your liking. This is a frightening revelation to young people (and is often learned the hard way), but it is the truth. Understand now and never forget that this is the era of self-reliance. Direct your own career. Success will come easier to those who practice self-initiative and self- management.

HAVE A NO-NONSENSE ATTITUDE

The uncertain world requires every young person to begin early in setting preliminary goals and in defining a personal philosophy of life. Don't just "drift along" as so many young people do. The job market demands excellence and commitment. Employers are unforgiving to those not having appropriate basic skills, technical abilities, general aptitudes, and proper motivation.

Begin developing a no-nonsense attitude about who you are, what you have going for you, and how you fit into the job market you wish to penetrate. This requires honest self-appraisal. For the next several years you will still be asking yourself these same questions. Keep in mind what Albert Einstein said: "Education is what you learn after you have forgotten everything you learned in school."

WHAT TO DO FIRST

There are other tough issues you must begin addressing up front: *Where do I want to go in life? What do I want to do with myself? What do I have to offer an employer? How will I get to my career destination? What will it take to accomplish my goals?*

First, think of a career as a never ending growth process, consisting of several stages. You will likely spend the rest of your life answering (and often struggling with) career-related questions. Don't worry that you can't see very far down the road right now.

Second, don't count on staying with the same organization for a lifetime. Not only will you change jobs at least five to six times, you will likely experience a variety of different careers in the process. Some job or career changes will happen because of your decision to change, while others will occur due to conditions beyond your control. Whatever the reason, don't let frequent job changes lower your self-esteem. Keep your bearings. Understanding the nature of career change will prevent "career shock."

Third, the content of each job held will change substantially several times. Technical breakthroughs will require continual retraining, retooling, updating, and skill-polishing as a matter of routine. The key here is to avoid "obsolescence shock."

It is absolutely essential for you to keep on top of these three points. Always be alert and responsive to change — don't be threatened by it. Growing in your career means learning, and the learning process must never end. You are finished if you stop developing your job-related abilities or quit expanding your career horizons. It's that simple. You either grow or die.

ESTABLISHING A THREE-YEAR GAME PLAN

Failing to plan means planning to fail. Getting a career started can be accomplished by preparing a three-year plan and reviewing it every three years (see Appendix for details). This short-term approach helps you stick your toe in the water before fully committing to a career path.

Do not be overly concerned beyond three years. Focus all your energies on the short-term and get going. At the end of the first or second year, roll your planning horizon out by a year or two.

Always stick with a three-year personal planning cycle. Why? It is simply too difficult to see clearly beyond that time. Most experienced business people or economists can't see much further out with clarity, so why should you? Besides, as a career beginner, you are testing vocational interests and career preferences. Reality probably will be different from expectations. Find out for sure and decide what to do about it. That's the best goal to set for your first three-year plan. You have enough to worry about. Don't compound your problems. Take the world a step at a time.

Understand that it might take two or three years to fully develop an accurate assessment of your vocational likes and dislikes. Just because you majored in a specific area doesn't mean you will enjoy the work once on the job full time. Too often, young people select vocational area and college programs for all the wrong reasons.

The first job in a chosen area might prove to be a big mistake. For many it is. To find out, assess it by these measures: *skills actually used, duties actually performed, sense of satisfaction and achievement, people with whom you associate, how the future looks, and your overall "gut feelings" about what you're doing, compared to expectations.* If you deal with these issues honestly and openly, making adjustments when needed, your future will have a better chance of working for you.

DEVELOP A VALUE SYSTEM

Begin your career search for excitement, challenge, financial rewards, and self-fulfillment with a solid philosophical frame of reference. Start to identify the principles which will guide your thinking about honesty, integrity, character, and forthrightness. Test your work ethic. Ask yourself: "Do I even have one?" These qualities will be significant assets in the future if you establish them now and stay true to them.

SET A SUSTAINABLE PACE

A key word to remember is "sustain." Develop an early pace that stretches you — but which is sustainable. This prevents early burnout and minimizes boredom. In the long term, your objective should be to work steadily to reach your potential. Right now, however, try to discover how much potential you really have and how you want to apply it over the long haul. This will come with time, experience, and the leadership you receive.

In the meantime, don't let complicated issues and concerns get in your way. Be patient. Remain flexible. Stay alert. Do not become frustrated. Stick to the fundamentals of getting started.

MENTORS

A mentor is someone willing to share the practical information necessary for you to be successful at various career stages. Their wisdom is based on their own business or professional background, personal experiences, and seasoned observations.

Identify, cultivate, and stay in touch with qualified mentors who can teach you what it takes to develop yourself. Carefully chosen mentors can also be role models and sources of moral support. Good mentors have proven success in their careers, maturity, a variety of career experiences to draw on, and savvy. Good mentors are caring and patient.

Seek a mentor's wise counsel, not just affirmation. Test career ideas on your mentor and listen with respect to the responses. Ask your mentor to be tough, to help examine your strengths and weaknesses in relation to your goals. Ask your mentor to compare your qualities to those you will be competing with. Always be honest with yourself in handling the information mentors share with you. A good mentor will brag on you and scold you as needed. If this candid relationship doesn't exist, you don't have a good mentor.

LEARNING ABOUT YOURSELF

Develop the right formula to succeed in the first job. Keep in mind that as life unfolds you will learn more about yourself, and you will be both pleasantly and unpleasantly surprised. You will be reinforced and encouraged. You will also suffer pain and disappointment, but your abilities will grow as you experience the "hard knocks" life of working. You will also receive much new information about career opportunities.

The biggest obstacle to overcome in career planning and personal goal setting is yourself, particularly your attitudes and feelings of inadequacy. Many fall into a trap of assuming that other people are better or are superior, when in fact others have the same feelings about you! Believe in yourself, and deal forcefully with the issue of self-confidence.

Growth, development, and fulfillment over a lifetime require vision, inquisitiveness, and resiliance. Do not get "down on yourself" or let frustration take control. Begin now to think honestly and analytically about who you are, where you want to go, what it will take to get you there, and (after you get there) whether you are where you really want to be. Approach the next few years as a time of exploration.

THE ROAD TO DISCOVERY

How do you feel about yourself? Do you have self-discipline and self-determination? Identify the tools you have to work with: your feelings of self-worth and self-confidence, and your sense of responsibility. You probably have much more going for you than you realize.

Take this self-analysis drill: List everything you can think of about yourself on a piece of paper. Group your strengths and weaknesses. Rank them in value based on mentors' advice, discussions with placement personnel and teachers, current job placement materials, and career planning literature. Then begin to build on your assets, striving to use each to its full advantage. Deal with your shortcomings. Be aggressive. Review your progress on a regular basis. Fully understand all aspects of developing leads, making contacts, and penetrating the job market. Find out what's important and what's not. Most of all, learn by doing.

You may ask, *"How do I begin?"* The answer is, you begin by beginning. Don't worry about false starts or early failures. It's *not* doing and missing the opportunity that is bad. Early career experiences are good lessons. Build on each experience and be a better person as a result. Above all, always feel good about yourself. If you don't feel good about yourself, you must deal with this feeling *immediately*.

JOB OUTLOOK IS CLOUDY

America's employment picture is difficult to pinpoint. College graduates and others entering the job market are caught in a crunch between several opposing forces that shape the demands of an employer. These include: a far-reaching corporate restructuring movement, heightened worldwide competition, rapidly changing technology, growing service industry, movement from the baby boom to baby bust generation, increased life expectancy, greater influx of foreigners, larger labor participation rates, and growing adult illiteracy as the gap between job skills needed and job skills possessed widens.

One of the most important parts of career planning is locating occupational information that is specific, timely, accurate, and useful. Keep in touch with employment services at federal, state, and local levels to determine the latest hiring trends, occupational developments, emerging skills requirements, and other job market information.

DO YOUR RESEARCH

Contact the U. S. Department of Labor, state departments of employment security, and local public and private job placement organizations. Get on their mailing lists for career and job outlook publications. Never assume that jobs and skills currently "hot" will continue to be so later on. Don't get caught in a trend that's peaking. Get in touch with reliable professional and trade associations supplying specific employment statistics and career outlook forecasts for jobs of interest to you. Stay on top of job trends based on your own vocational interests and geographical preferences.

Whatever the job market of the 1990's may be, young people who want career-oriented, entry-level positions can expect tough sledding. Obsolete industries and cost-cutting businesses are firing thousands of workers and managers a year. This unsettling trend will continue for the next few years. In the meantime, the country is awash with the resumés of trained, experienced — but displaced — managers and technicians.

WHERE ARE THE JOBS?

Don't misunderstand — there will be plenty of work. Over two million new jobs are currently created every year in this country. New jobs are being generated at a rate faster than our population is growing.

But most new jobs (about two-thirds of them) are in small businesses. Nearly 90 percent are in service industries, with less than 10 percent in manufacturing. The bad news for college graduates is that 40 percent of all new service industry jobs now being created are near minimum wage levels. Some forecasters suggest that by the year 2000, nearly 80 percent of all new jobs will be in "low-tech" or "no-tech" service categories. Many will not pay well and most will not have sufficient content to challenge or offer career potential.

Do not look for the high-tech job movement, given so much play in the business and economic press, to account for much more than from 10 to 20 percent of all new jobs created each year until around the year 2000. This new technology wave is still cranking up and needs a few years of investment capital accumulation and market development to get rolling full steam. Furthermore, most future employment opportunities, perhaps from 80 to 90 percent of them, will be in metropolitan areas. Very little new job-creating activity will likely occur in rural America.

Larger corporations, particularly Fortune 500 firms, will be a poor source of employment for college graduates until the restructuring now taking place is over. If anything, the "cutting back" movement, including the abolishment of entire layers of management and dramatic reductions in administrative support staff, is picking up steam among smaller companies. A return to higher inflation and economic sluggishness in the years ahead will seriously complicate matters for many college-trained career beginners.

WHAT ABOUT 18 YEAR-OLDS?

Entry-level job opportunities for 18 year olds will abound. Businesses, colleges and universities, and military services will compete intensely for these people if they are qualified and trainable. This is due to a smaller number of employable 18 year olds than in years past. That's what the "baby bust" generation is all about. But to be successful in this entry-level job market, job hunters must have increasingly higher levels of analytical and communication skills, literacy levels above simple reading and writing ability, solid maturity, openness to continual instruction and retraining, and job mobility. Those with the skills and the willingness to go where the jobs are have a clear edge for career beginnings and growth.

OPENING THE DOORS

One more thing: Good grades show competence but will not be the only key to finding a job. Interpersonal skills, school activities, and campus leadership qualities will also be valuable. Think about these trade-offs. Either way, you must demonstrate individual growth potential and have sufficient personal strengths to get somebody's attention and sell yourself. Otherwise, you may have a serious problem from the beginning. Do not become a dinosaur with obsolete goals, poor skills, or a bad attitude early in your career.

Even with the necessary qualifications, it may take six months or longer of intense interviewing and searching to find what you want. Strong individual effort beyond college placement offices may be necessary. Patience is another necessity. Never become discouraged. Keep trying!

GETTING STARTED IN CAREER

These 34 recommendations are especially designed for college students and other career beginners preparing to embark. See for yourself where you stack up on the basic issues that will make a difference in getting the right job or in beginning your career on the right foot.

1. *Yes, there is life after college. Resolve to be precisely what you want to be as a person.* Think as big as you dare with the size of your ambition and goals as a starting point. Get somebody's attention, then deliver. Perform on the job to the best of your ability.

2. *Lead from your strengths. Seek a precise understanding of your abilities and your aptitudes — what excites you.* Build on the inventory of experiences you have developed. Understand your weaknesses and identify anything holding you back. Correct them if you can, and as you

can, but don't dwell on them — this saps your energy and gets in the way.

3. *Get plenty of career information from a variety of sources, but be sure you seek advice from people who are qualified.* Be careful of people who might have a narrow interest or biased reasons for steering you in one direction or another. Get second and third opinions. It might be wise to spend a few hundred dollars getting advice from a carefully chosen and professionally certified career counselor.

4. *Avoid locking into one narrow occupation, tied to your major field of study or resulting from advice of parents or peers.* This one-option approach could be a blind alley leading nowhere. Develop alternatives. Understand trade-offs. There is no perfect job. Be flexible. Remember, you are just getting started. Don't stampede into a quick job search. Don't be in a hurry to commit once you receive an offer. Instead, explore a variety of employment opportunities. Then decide.

5. *Be careful that you don't get yesterday's advice about tomorrow's jobs.* Sources of advice may or may not be reliable. Changes in the job market are happening so quickly that too many people have their view of the world linked to the past or to where they are, and to where they will likely stay. They are unable to sense the future where you must go. Your minister, home town business leader, or family friend may be totally out of touch with career opportunities outside your community. That's why you need a variety of advice.

6. *Do not accept career advice from anyone who had a bad Depression-related experience.* They never forget. These people are typically super-cautious and maintain a bird-in-hand approach to the world. Their advice will be: "Don't be reckless. Take a job and stick with it. Focus on security. Stay put." This is molasses-flow advice in a lightning-fast world. Don't get mired down.

7. *As a hard and fast rule, your objective in early jobs is to learn. Get experiences, not security.* It's much too soon to be concerned about pensions and long-range benefits. Focus on learning something that will contribute toward long-term career growth.

8. *Keep a positive attitude toward instruction and training. You must be trainable.* But more important, you must have willingness to accept training (not everyone does). Don't seek employment until you are planted squarely at this point. If you can't accept instruction or job-related advice from supervisors, you will simply waste your time.

9. *Be responsible.* For example, you will be expected to: show up

on schedule; be presentable in appearance; maintain a positive attitude while there; and have the self-discipline to stay on the job. If you aren't ready to accept these basic responsibilities, don't apply. Instead, get your head together. Put first things first.

10. *Make sure you have communication skills.* Can you write a letter containing complete sentences and correctly spelled words? Can you speak effectively? If you can't read, write, spell, and communicate, take remedial work now. You cannot hide this deficiency for long. Poor communication skills will drag you down. If you don't know how you stack up, ask teachers who will tell you the truth.

11. *Know your stuff.* Success is 50 percent what you know. That's content! The other 50 percent is in how you tell what you know. That's communication! To excel, you must have both *knowledge* and *communication ability.* If you don't have both of these vital qualities, you have serious problems.

12. *Place value on other basic skills as well: mathematical, analytical, rational, and computational abilities are very important.* Are you sure you can understand technical reports, comprehend computer instructions, operate complex equipment? Can you think logically? Are you absolutely sure? If not, do something about it now.

13. *Math is important.* If you are weak in math you will be forever eliminated from two-thirds of the higher skilled, technology-based, better paying jobs available. If math is a weakness, an additional year or two concentrating on math concepts to strengthen them might be a sound investment if you have the aptitude and will-power. Talk to math professors. Perhaps take evening school courses. If you are hopelessly weak in math, don't be discouraged. Other fields offer challenging potential. The key is to seek them out.

14. *Focus attention and energies on job opportunities in which you have a realistic chance to succeed.* Don't be distracted by pipe dreams and fantasy goals.

15. *Don't let pride or embarrassment hinder your marketability to prospective employers.* Most of all, do not kid yourself into thinking you will be successful if you don't have the basic tools. You can't bluff your way through life. Deal with this before you seek or accept a specific job.

16. *Today's workplace is a tough arena for young people.* You have absolutely no guarantees, no assurances, and no blanket protection.

17. *Remember that all you have is the opportunity.* Grow to your full potential. Two great social wastes of our time are *lost opportunity*

and *unfulfilled potential.* Many young people have never learned this lesson. They don't realize that ultimately, getting the job done, making it in a tough, competitive world, is entirely up to them. The world becomes a little bit lonely at this point. Have courage!

18. *If you are suddenly getting weak in the knees, remember that it is never too late to turn things around.* If you are near graduation — and you feel as though you have wasted your college years — don't panic. You still have plenty of time — about 50 years. Stop and regroup. Talk to several people at school whom you trust: your advisor, department head, dean, or even the college president. Seek out mentors. Get a variety of opinions. If necessary, take an extra year or two to get whatever preparation you need. This bold step may require you to continue your education on a part-time basis while holding down an interim job. But do it! At all costs, even if you have to finance the tuition, get yourself qualified to compete long term in the job market of your choice.

19. *Forget acceptance by others as a goal. Ignore peer pressure.* Lesser humans, those without goals and potential, desire and covet acceptance, but this should not be enough for you. Set your sights on greatness. Pursue accomplishment. Reach toward the mountain top. Seek or accept no advice from anyone who doesn't have his own act together.

20. *Beware of well-meaning but out-of-touch parents.* If your parents want you to be an engineer and you want to make it as a social worker or public school teacher, don't try to please them and be miserable. Go for it. Tell them you love them, respect them, and appreciate everything they have done for you but engineering isn't what you want. After all, it is your life, and you have to live it your way.

21. *Help your parents.* Parents have an obligation to prepare you to fly from the nest, not to keep you in it. If they forget this important point, remind them. Parents should spend their time letting go, even if it's little by little. The problem is that many parents have not fully accepted this philosophy of letting teen-agers grow up. Be patient and demonstrate understanding as you teach parents the facts of life. The other side of the coin is whether or not you are ready to fly from the nest.

22. *Do not burn bridges at home, in the workplace, or with faculty at school.* You may need a good reference. You may also need a place to sleep, a place for advice, or a place to cry. To succeed in life you will need organized assistance at every step along the way. Support groups are important. Most of all, you will always need a friend. In fact, parents

may be the best friends you will ever have. Don't overlook this. Always be able to communicate with them and to go home.

23. *Regardless of circumstances, if things don't go right, stop!* Gain full control of yourself and your job situation. Listen carefully to voices deep inside. Look with penetrating eyes at the face in the mirror. Be honest. If you don't like what you see, do what's necessary to take corrective action. Get comfortable with yourself so you can move toward a fulfilling career and a happy life.

24. *If you are an older career beginner, whatever your age, it's never too late to stop, take stock, and seek new direction for your life.* If you must find a job, do not be victimized by peer pressure from neighbors, former schoolmates, family, friends, or other contacts. Most of your associates are only acquaintances — not long-term friends. When it comes to making career decisions, they don't really matter. Be assertive, self-confident, and independent. Do what you want to do. More importantly, do what you have to do. Stay in charge.

25. *Never be miserable in a job. It is self-defeating.* Frustration destroys ambition and self-worth. It leads to bad habits and crutches, such as drugs or alcohol. Don't fall into the trap of negative thinking.

26. *Take your career one step at a time.* If you take a job or enter a training program, give it a fair chance. But if you are absolutely sure the job isn't right for you, don't waste your time or their money. Make these decisions carefully and with counseling. If you leave your employer, do so on a professional level with class, dignity, and by their rules.

27. *Make sound decisions.* If you are in your early 20s, statistically you have approximately 60 years to live. Right now, you are laying the framework for how you will earn a living for a long period of time. You are deciding on a career path and how to make something out of yourself. Perhaps you are even considering your financial ability to support a family. In assessing these matters, don't minimize the consequences of immature decisions and irresponsible actions on future career development. Make sure you know what you are doing. Can you shoulder the financial requirements, work responsibilities, and personal commitments required? If you haven't already faced these issues with a sense of maturity, grow up.

28. *As you plan your future and begin to work your plan, stop every few months for a self-appraisal.* Seek the truth that hurts, not the truth that sets you free. As you analyze your progress (or lack of it), seek reasons and understanding, not affirmation that gives you false reinfor-

cement. Try not to become discouraged. You are in a learning process with a long way to go, so be patient! Keep clear-headed about what you want.

29. *Begin immediately to practice money management.* Saving money is the key to career flexibility and exploiting job opportunities. Ask bankers and other financial planners about the magic of interest-compounding and what saving a few dollars on a regular basis will mean later.

Put money into a rainy day fund equivalent to the amount of cash you need to survive for six months should you suddenly find yourself unemployed.

Begin an individual retirement account (IRA) as soon as possible. The importance of this cannot be overstated, especially looking back 10-15 years later, at what could have been. Personal financial security is the foundation for independence. Never depend exclusively on Social Security or a company pension for your retirement.

30. *Attention, please!* Contrary to peer pressure and advertisers, you do not have to invest your first year's wages in a sports car, personal computer, exotic vacation, VCR, and fancy clothes. It's smart to save from the very beginning, even if you have to sacrifice. Do not start spending money you expect to make before you earn it. Be careful of "no money down" or "first time buyers" promotions aimed at college graduates. Wait until you get at least six months of work at the same place of employment under your belt before you incur any real debt. What would you do about monthly installment payments if you decide, or your employer should decide, your job is not suited for you?

31. *Do not let job titles, glamorous sounding professions, impressive salary levels, and material appearances of the so- called "yuppie" generation seduce you.* Thousands of Americans under 40 are suffering from job stress and emotional problems. While seeming to have it all — title, prestige, money, power — on the inside, many young people are very unhappy. Money can't buy happiness and satisfaction. Think about life on a deeper level. Don't start at the wrong place in making job commitments and obligating yourself. Look beyond the glitter. Real happiness is not found in things.

32. *What about an advanced degree?* This is a crucial question without an obvious answer. My strong recommendation is to work a minimum of two years in a job after receiving an undergraduate degree. This experience will provide a good perspective on the value of future

graduate work. Advice from a variety of respected sources is important. I raise this red flag to prevent you from investing thousands of dollars and several years pursuing graduate education and professional certification in an area that might be frustrating and unrewarding.

There is a limit to classroom learning before experiencing a job first-hand. Remember the saying? "Try it, you might like it." The other side is, "Try it, you might find out that you don't like it." Determine which is true as early as possible. You do this on the job, not in the classroom. Before you commit to another layer of education, take a second or third look at what you will be getting into: time commitment, stress, emotional strain, energy drain, and what you give up in family relations and reduced social life. And when seeking advice, professors may be biased about attending graduate school, particularly if you have good grades and are considering their school. For balance, also talk to recent graduates of programs that interest you.

33. *Let me make this critical point one more time: As you prepare to take your first job, minimize the rude awakening called "reality shock."* As previously pointed out, there is a gap between career beginners' expectations and actual day-to-day experience. Issues such as daily duties, personalities, supervisor's leadership abilities and management styles, on-the-job behaviors, rules and procedures, dress codes, as well as training and professional growth potential can never be adequately described by job recruiters or potential employers.

Many people interviewing you for a job will overstate the immediate challenge, potential, and opportunities. As a result, there is a conflict between reality and what you expect. You may feel little sense of satisfaction, contribution, or belonging to the organization, but you must experience reality on the job to determine if early career expectations are being met. If after giving the job a fair chance you still don't like it -- leave, it won't get any better.

34. *If you have experimented with drugs, stop.* If you are into drugs regularly, seek help now. If you are using alcohol excessively, deal with your problem. This cancer which is destroying so many useful young lives will consume you as well. If you are clean — be careful. Assist others who might need help. Positive peer pressure works best. Keep in mind that two-thirds of all young people entering the work force today have used illegal drugs at some point. This means you do need to be careful in choosing your associates. Be alert to their intentions. Stay away from those who would drag you down so they can crawl over you in the com-

petition for promotion, or, because of their own failure, would seek gratification in lowering you to their level. Keep in mind that more companies, especially larger corporations, are requiring drug testing as part of the hiring process. Don't fail this entrance exam and ruin your career before getting started.

SPECIAL MESSAGE TO WOMEN AND MINORITIES

Good news! Social rules, cultural norms, recent court decisions, and political pressures for affirmative action are continuing to break down barriers and open up career-oriented jobs in corporate management ranks for women and minorities. The bad news is that fields and positions historically occupied by men in America's larger corporations may be resistant to change.

Unfortunately, the male prejudice is surviving the corporate restructuring movement now taking place in our business system. The advancement of women and minorities is likely to be slow because entire levels of middle-management and above are disappearing on a wholesale basis. Expansion of management and support positions at the volume experienced in the 1960's and 1970's will not be forthcoming in the 1990's. This situation bears watching by all.

Careful occupational planning coupled with mobility will be crucial to women and minorities seeking to enhance their careers. The 1990's will be a period of uncertainty and unpredictability for those having to mount social and cultural barriers in pursuit of a career. It will be important to look at entrepreneurial opportunities as an alternative in America's quickly changing workplace. But be sure to carefully review the information contained in Chapter Thirteen before deciding whether to invest or get involved with others in a small business venture. Not only are there substantial financial risks, there are other considerations — leadership styles, time commitments, and work requirements in entrepreneurial firms aren't for everyone.

DON'T BE A DINOSAUR

George Bernard Shaw has some strong advice. *"Take care to get what you like or you will be forced to like what you get."* According to Fred Smith, noted businessman, author, and lecturer, "We accept our right to choose attitudes, occupations, and relations, knowing full well we may be free to act, but not free from the consequences of our act." In short, we can't have it both ways. The freedom of choice carries accountability for our decisions. This is why you must take responsibility for your life and take charge from the beginning. Do not be a sheep in the herd.

Consider advice about attitudes from golfer Arnold Palmer: "If you think you can or if you think you can't, either way, you are probably right." Always think that you can. And to keep you humble the morning after graduation, Fred Smith also advises, "Those who feel they are educated at graduation will slowly turn into disposable dinosaurs." His message is that if you are just graduating from college, you have only just begun. You will live and work in a life-long classroom.

CAREER STARTER CHECKLIST

Start now to pull together your career plan, but don't just focus narrowly on job skills and pay checks. Include these basics:

- Learn to manage your time wisely.
- Develop ways to manage the inevitable stresses of life and work.
- Develop a personal financial plan.
- Maintain physical fitness.
- Cultivate your spiritual life.
- Make your career work for you so more opportunity will come your way.
- Grow to your potential.
- Remember that the smarter you work now, the luckier you will be later on.

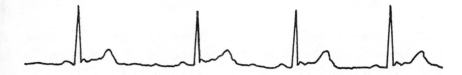

9

UNDER THIRTY? LISTEN CLOSELY!

While you live in the present, look to the future. There is a time for you to work and a time for you to play; a time for you to plan and a time for you to learn.

If you have been in your career for five years or so, here's a personal challenge: Stop for a moment to think clearly about where you are headed in your job and career. Are you going in the right direction? Are you absolutely sure? How are you measuring your progress? What are your priorities?

Have you ever taken the time to identify what really matters to you? Do your motivations make sense? Or are you driven by surface needs and superficial desires? Are you solely concentrating on today in how you spend your time and money? Are you letting your future take care of itself?

Are you paying attention to the component of your life that has to do with basic beliefs, ethical standards, and spiritual values?

Do you know what's happening in the outside world around you? Have you been thinking seriously about the implications of dramatic changes now taking place in America's workplace at every level and in all industries and professions?

Deal with these changes. Determine your stake in them. Assess their likely impact, not only on your current occupation, but on your future as well. Could bad things happen to you?

Seize opportunity. Capitalize on change by building on your job-related strengths and correcting weaknesses that could impede your growth.

Reposition yourself for tomorrow through intelligent goal-setting, determining priorities based on what's really important, and by careful marketing of your skills. Gain a competitive advantage and claim your share of the future.

Keep in mind that a shocking number of young professionals with glamorous titles and big salaries are finding themselves unfulfilled, unchallenged, and short on inner satisfaction. According to psychologist Douglas LaBier, part of the problem has to do with working in a stifling corporate structure, realizing that a job has become a treadmill existence, or with conflicts that develop between human values and what it takes to be successful today.[4]

If your career profile is one of frustration, boredom, or helplessness, if you want to prevent "career shock," the following candid advice will hold special meaning.

26 RECOMMENDATIONS WITH YOU IN MIND

1. *Self-reliance and self-management are of primary importance to your career success.* The self-factors developed in Chapter Seven apply to you. Remember, no one will take care of you or assure your future. You must take charge of what you want to be, accept full accountability for what you are, and assume responsibility for what you become. Keep in mind that you are all that you have. Manage yourself wisely. Remember that time is working for you right now. Don't waste it.

2. *Future job uncertainties demand that you develop a three-year strategic plan.* Do this even if things are going well (for detailed information on three-year career reviews, see Appendix). Not only must you have a three-year plan with clear cut goals — goals which are measurable, attainable, and time-bound — you must also have the self-discipline to work the plan. Don't be victimized by procrastination or sidetracked by good intentions. Develop a priority checklist, but don't focus narrowly on job and promotions. Look deeper at basic beliefs and values. Examine yourself from a spiritual perspective, as a whole person. Be able to believe in yourself. Don't ignore this dimension of your life — you might be missing the key to your future.

3. *How do you measure up on thinking, communicating, and organizational skills?* Make an honest evaluation of your competency level in these six basic skills.

- Can you communicate effectively?
- Can you write letters, memos, and reports for impact and for a favorable response?
- Can you read for comprehension at the technical level many jobs require?
- Can you think logically and analytically?
- Do you have good speaking and listening skills?
- Do you have time utilization and organizational skills?

If you have weaknesses in any of these areas, do something about them now. They won't go away. They will become even greater stumbling blocks to gaining recognition and getting those promotions you seek. For example, as you go further up the responsibility ladder, poor communication and organizational skills will become greater obstacles. If you can't communicate effectively, or carry out your assignment in a timely manner, you will likely peak out prematurely based on self-inflicted damage.

Poor communication and bad time management simply turn people off. Weak communication skills work against you through the Peter Principle: You will rise to your highest level of incompetence as measured by those above you. On the positive side, even if you are self-confident about your skill level in these vital areas, can you do even better? Keep a sharp edge on each skill. Don't forget the concert pianist, the world-class sprinter, and the all-American athlete have three things in common: practice, practice, and practice. Being the best, whatever the field, requires suffering the pain of self-discipline and preparation.

4. *Stay abreast of what it takes technically to do your job effectively.* Skill obsolescence is becoming rampant. Make sure you do this yourself — don't wait for somebody to do it for you. Staying abreast requires spending your available time wisely, with a good portion allocated to professional development efforts, technical seminars, and basic skills refresher courses. Capitalize on skills-development opportunities, even if you have to pay out of your own pocket. Look at continuing education as a wise investment.

5. *Establish your own ethical rules and standards by which to operate.* There's too much sleaze and hypocrisy today. Reject it. Compromise with your business associates only if you think they are operat-

ing ethically and morally on high ground. Decide early the ground rules you will apply for conducting your business affairs. The acid test is your own internal test of self-respect. If you haven't begun to deal with these philosophical issues, you are still immature regardless of your age. Start growing up. Face them now so you will be able to deal effectively with challenges to your ethical standards later on. Know where you stand on these fundamental questions before you are confronted with threats. Remember the ancient biblical wisdom: "A good name is better than fine perfume." (Ecclesiastes 7:1, NIV)

6. *Always negotiate your future with your organization at the beginning of your relationship and on a current basis.* Approach your employment arrangement one year at a time. Take care of yourself first. Lead from your strengths. Be as firm as you choose in striking your deal with your employer. The mentality of the marketplace increasingly requires and rewards negotiating persistence on your part. Don't leave any bargaining chips on the table.

7. *Don't fall for corporate seduction — the hollow promise of long-term career opportunities, future rewards, and long-range benefits.* Your employer knows he probably won't have to pay off because chances are you won't be there to collect. He knows the odds at the beginning. Ask people in the human resources department how pension funds are calculated: They will tell you that substantial employee turnover is factored in all the way. Pension fund managers are betting on substanial employee turnover in calculating future liabilities. That's why a growing number of companies are offering non-contributory pension plans. Actually, you'd be much better off working for an organization that requires you to pay half your retirement. At least, you'd have something to show for your time if you had to leave prematurely.

8. *Earn your pay.* Be an outstanding performer. Do your job thoroughly, professionally, with pride and dignity. Give your employer a full measure of what you have to offer every day. This approach can offset the poor management you might be experiencing, and old-fashioned work values might also lead to tomorrow's promotion. This is particularly true if your boss sets goals for you, gives you feedback, and helps you through counseling and coaching. If you aren't working in an organization where goals and feedback are a normal part of the management process, ask your supervisors to start them. This will let you know where you stand and what it takes to be a top performer.

9. *Spend time working in professional associations and community*

organizations. While it is self-serving, build your network of contacts for the future. A career growth strategy requires organized assistance in getting from where you are now to where you might want to go in the future.

10. *Find a sponsor where you work.* Most highly successful people in large organizations have benefited from a sponsor. The sponsor is someone up the organizational ladder who serves as your ambassador by keeping you before the management hierarchy. The sponsor is the person who will plead your case for promotions with decision makers at the top. If your goal is growth and advancement within the organization, you need to cultivate such a person. Believe me, there is much truth to the principle: "It's not always what you know, it's who you know that counts."

11. *Have a mentor to guide you.* You should also start courting a key person, successful in business or a profession, with impeccable credentials to be your mentor. This mentor should be called on to guide you and to coach you. Cultivate someone in your community, outside the organization where you work, whom you trust and respect. The mentor is a person you regard with deep respect. This person need not be a friend. Rather, he or she is a teacher. Select someone who will be truthful, even if it hurts, when giving advice designed to help you develop the skills important to you.

12. *Begin immediately to develop a personal financial strategy.* Do not let anything — *anything* — stand in the way of building a protective financial cushion for short-term contingencies and long-term security. This step is a must for mid-career flexibility. Take my word for it, you probably won't always be with the same organization. Discount your employer's pension plan completely in your thinking. Instead, you need to begin now building a personal retirement fund.

13. *Establish a minimum six month rainy day fund for emergencies.* This provides protection if you are fired, laid off, or want to quit but don't have the financial resources to tide you over. Every responsible job counselor will tell you to stick with your job until you find another. This is good advice and is becoming even more important, but if you ever have to bail out, or are thrown out, you must have the financial reserves to carry you so you can look for another job without panicking. If you have resumé skills, the secret to mobility and flexibility in the workplace is savings!

14. *Start a long-term financial program.* Each year, put as much

money as possible in an Individual Retirement Account (IRA) or similar long-term interest tax sheltered investment. If possible, put aside the maximum allowed, currently $2,000. Do it by payroll deduction or by electronic funds transfer at your personal financial institution. Another approach is by lump sum payment. But do it, regardless of whether you can take a tax deduction for any part of the amount you set aside. Years down the road, this will be the best financial favor you have ever done for yourself. Why? Ask your banker or broker for a calculation to age 65 of your investment in an IRA and see the magic of compound interest. The key is to start early in life. For example, beginning at age 22, if you put aside $2.000 per year for six years, at 12% interest, your IRA at age 65 would be worth $1.3 million. That's a $12,000 investment made early and left alone. Think about it.

15. *Make tough financial choices.* At this point, you are lamenting you can't afford to put money aside for future financial security. If this is the case, postpone buying the BMW or fancy car until much later. Cut your ski trips in half. Quit buying the $100 shirts and blouses. Make do with less. Delay, postpone, and be frugal! Who are you trying to impress with designer clothes, fancy cars, and trendy condos? Who do you think cares what you wear or drive or where you take vacations? The answer? Nobody. You're just feeding your own ego. Instead, put together a few basic clothing sets and interchange. Be reasonable on transportation and lodging. Apply self-restraint. Think about tomorrow, not just about living for today.

16. Let me backtrack a bit. I am not knocking appearances. I believe very strongly in the value of professional apparel and sharp but tasteful attire. *Dressing for success is extremely important, along with appropriate grooming. Just use good judgment.*

17. *Deal with differences between career expectations and career realities.* What I mean is that as you make your way through the early years of your professional life, you will be developing experience and maturity. You aren't born with these: You acquire them the hard way. In the process, you might find you have made a mistake in your choice of jobs or profession. Because of a lack of fulfillment and challenge in your work, you might need to back off and regroup. You might even be asked to leave your place of employment. Because of these uncertainties, you must be flexible in your lifestyle.

As a general rule, do not make financial commitments today based on your optimistic hope for tomorrow's salary growth. Do not spend the money you haven't earned. In short, with respect to financial planning on the income side, do not live in the future. Do not project what your future income will likely be and ignore future liabilities when making commitments for major purchases. Instead, deal with realities. Understand that the financial equation has two sides: income and outgo. Do not live beyond your income. Spend according to current income levels. Doing otherwise is a high risk approach that can lead to personal financial disaster later on.

Be especially careful of buying a house or condo early in life assuming that you can recoup your investment through steady property appreciation. Some of the traps are that the immediate market can overbuild, construction can be shabby, and plant layoffs or a sour economy in general can drop the bottom out of the local housing market. Also, keep in mind that because of tax reform you can't benefit from long-term tax gains. I'm not saying *not* to buy property, just to be very careful in doing so. Consider whether you will be in the same job or even in the same geographical area for long enough to warrant the risk.

You should not go off the deep end early in your career with heavy debts for cars, clothes, and other personal possessions. Sizable monthly payments will chain you to your present situation. Don't get stuck in this quagmire. That's why you should plan three years at a time. This time frame keeps all possibilities in front of you. Unpleasant surprises are minimized.

18. *Be careful of the people with whom you associate on the job.* Many individuals exist whose intentions are not honorable. There are those who will try to drag you down by wasting your time, poisoning your enthusiasm, and dampening your spirit. This is especially true if you are star potential. You may be seen as a competitive threat to your colleagues! These people are your enemies, and this is their strategy for soothing their own deficiencies. Keep your distance from people who are negative or constant complainers. Do not associate with people who can't challenge you spiritually and intellectually. You can easily recognize the type. Many of them linger around water fountains and office copiers. They take extended coffee breaks or lunch hours. They also meet after hours in bars to complain about fellow employees, company policies, and decisions being made at the office. They aren't enthusiastic or committed. They aren't on the team and are detrimental to the organization's future success.

19. *Develop a professional growth attitude about yourself that tempts*

you to greatness. Focus on excellence. If you desire the best for yourself in your own professional life, you must understand that achievement does not come to most people by accident. You must be technically competent, self-disciplined, and maintain a professional attitude. In addition, you must also learn how to develop a healthy relationship with others. Relating to your colleagues and being a positive influence to them are powerful leadership qualities.[5]

20. *Pick heroes and role models carefully.* Learn the difference between envy and respect. Many people confuse the two. Think about it. You may envy someone's success as measured by title, power, cars, or clothes; but do you have respect for that person? Don't take the wrong cues and, for the wrong reasons, try to emulate someone whom you may envy, but actually disrespect.

21. *Be very careful of the "grass-is-greener" urge.* Do not be overly anxious to move or hop from job to job. It is interesting that most people who change jobs would not have chosen the organization they left if they had the decision to make again. Part of the reason many people are always disappointed is that they don't do their homework — they don't know why they are unhappy or restless. It could be symptomatic of our mobile, rootless society. My advice is to avoid being spontaneous or too quick in your decisions. Move deliberately, and only after careful planning. Do detailed research first. Ask candid questions. It's your life and you have a right to know.

If a new job is available elsewhere because someone has departed, find out specifically why he or she left before you accept the offer. Track down the person whose place you will be taking, and ask questions. Make sure you are not just trying to bail out of your own situation. Too many people with this motivation have jumped from the frying pan into the fire with deep regret. Moreover, there is no real evidence that people who change jobs frequently automatically improve their financial position or career prospects as a result. This is largely a myth.

22. *Beware of fast talking job recruiters.* One way of looking at a new job opportunity is what I call the "mystique versus reality" of the position. While the picture painted is very enticing, too often, job-hoppers have discovered that the new position is essentially more of the same. Rather than being a new challenge, the job typically settles down to the familiar old routine with the only difference being in the cast of characters. Don't end up experiencing the same job five different times. Keep in mind that job content, leadership style, and company policies

in different organizations can be strangely similar. The key is to break out of the cycle.

23. *Avoid job change unless it is a genuine improvement over your present situation.* Judge the new opportunity on more than just financial grounds. Look for appropriate job content based on your skills and interests. Carefully iron out authority and responsibility. Always seek intellectual stimulation. Most importantly, make sure future employers respect your personal dignity and self-esteem. Hopefully, you will be able to enjoy yourself. Work on it.

24. Again, and I repeat this because of its importance, *do not make a decision to leave your present job solely on the basis of a desire to escape.* If you are bailing out and don't do your homework, chances are your parachute won't open and you will take a hard fall. If so, you will be making an extremely bad mistake and will be sorry about your decision.

25. *On the subject of drugs and chemical abuse: Consider the words of David Crosby, rock star of the 60's:*

> I don't care who you are. It's not a matter of personality. Do them [drugs] and it's a matter of time before you are addicted. You can give me any rationalization you want, I know better. I have a Ph.D. in drugs. Fool with them and you'll get strung out. Take them and there are about four ways it can go: You can go crazy; you can go to prison; you can die; or, you can kick. That's it. Anything else anybody says is bull.[6]

26. *Make every step in your career journey work for you.* Apply brain power. Stay in charge. Do not let bad things happen to you because you lose control. Move in the direction dictated by your interests, career preferences, and abilities. Remain alert to all signs and signals of job change discussed in Chapter Six. Do not be overly influenced by peers or others who have no stake in your long-term emotional well-being. Don't do anything stupid you will regret later.

BEWARE OF TREADMILL SHOCK

Watch out for "treadmill shock," or job letdown. Said another way, it's reality overtaking career expectations in a negative sense. This feeling of disappointment and frustration happens anywhere from five to ten years out of school, when you realize that what you thought would be an exciting and meaningful career in a prestigious profession, or working for a glamorous organization, has really resulted in years of meaningless, boring work. Some jobs are exalted by society but end up being merely long days full of drudgery and monotony for most (except for those at the top). Many lawyers, accountants, dentists, engineers, and middle-level managers (who went to Harvard or Wharton expecting to arrive on the executive floor by age 30 or 35) find themselves instead floundering on a treadmill at 40. Don't be like them. Don't be victimized by treadmill shock.

UNDER THIRTY CHECKLIST

- Lead a balanced lifestyle.
- Be prepared with a practical three-year plan.
- Self-reliance and self-discipline are the keys to shaping your strategy.
- There is no short-cut or substitute for working smart.
- Success is usually determined by what happens from the shoulders up.
- Don't look for quick-fixes or easy answers.
- Prove to others and yourself that you have what it takes.
- Build your resumé on solid performance.
- Always give a full measure of yourself.
- Maintain financial flexibility. Have a rainy day fund. Begin your individual retirement program immediately.
- Carefully select your friends.
- Do not succumb to corporate seduction or the corporate medicine man.
- Negotiate your job arrangements.
- Prudently manage what you have: your ability, your time, your fitness, your inner being, your dollars, and your potential.

Hopefully, opportunities you deserve will follow. It's up to you to make it happen for you.

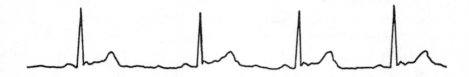

10

MID-LIFE OUGHT NOT
BE A CRISIS

You mistakenly think your mid-life crisis is to be kept in the closet, hidden from others. What you have is the potential for a new journey of discovery and fulfillment. The key is what you do about mid-life before it happens to you.

I am not a clinical expert on the psychological causes of mid-life dilemmas. However, many of the people with whom I talk about career issues who are in their late 30's or 40's have one common characteristic: faced with pressures for accomplishment, sensing a career plateau, or experiencing changes within their organizations that have blocked their growth paths, *they have become disenchanted, are puzzled, feel unchallenged, or experience frustration about their present work situation.*

MID-LIFE DOESN'T HAVE TO BE A CRISIS

In fact, a mid-life review of who you are, where you are now, where you are headed, and what you need to be doing in response is to be expected and is usually beneficial. Everyone goes through these self-examinations at some point. There is absolutely nothing wrong with experiencing one. With a career plan properly implemented, the sense of personal achievement and inner fulfillment for most should be at its greatest during mid-life years.

An objective assessment of where you are compared to where you really want to be may be the greatest event of your life. The mid-life years can be a time of continued growth or the beginning of a nightmare. What counts is how you anticipate the coming of "mid-life" and how you respond.

Unfortunately, this predictable, psychological mid-life phenomenon has too often been disguised as an inevitable crisis to be endured and survived. It is jokingly called the "middle-age crazies." Because of this attitude, most people hesitate to discuss mid-life feelings. Those with problems keep them under wraps. But the experience doesn't have to be bad. Here's why!

Much literature on mid-life crisis and how to deal with it has been written either by those who have undergone personal crisis, and want to share the bad news of their experience, or by professionals who have counseled patients suffering though severe mid-life dilemmas. As expected, the view is reinforced that, sometime between the ages of 35 and 45, every person *must* go through a wrenching, tear-jerking, traumatic crisis, often with dire consequences. Many people do, of course, but many others don't. And others who do experience a personal crisis could have avoided much of the agony if they had approached the issue differently.

One predictable characteristic of most is that they haven't really thought about the reasons for their unrest. Nearly all of them were unprepared mentally, emotionally, financially, and/or spiritually. Mid-career simply hit them by surprise. And this is the crucial point—why do so many people let crises related to career and personal circumstances catch them off guard and overtake their lives? Think about this question on a larger scale for a moment.

OTHER CRISIS POINTS IN LIFE

Parallels exist in several other so-called "crisis points." Somehow, even with the large amounts of literature now available on potential crisis situations adults confront, we seem never to be quite prepared for the following four situations.

1. Our *first job* is a definite crisis point. Never having experienced full-time employment, we don't fully understand what is about to happen to us or what will be expected of us. The picture painted by prospec-

tive employers and campus recruiters is far more glamorous than reality. Business school students in particular have a difficult time adjusting because in the classroom we are taught how to make executive decisions and solve all the world's problems. But on the job, instead of being called on by the chief executive officer or board of directors for our wisdom, we are handed a broom and told to sweep the floor.

"Reality shock" quickly sets in. Many young recruits and nearly half of all college graduates who enter corporate training programs leave within five years. When the real work world does not come close to matching personal expectations, disappointment quickly sets in. Unfortunately, early job experiences and first impressions about people with whom we must associate set the stage for shaping our attitudes toward future employers and career choices. Bad experiences have lingering negative consequences.

2. *Marriage* is a crisis point. Most people don't think through the seriousness of marriage. There is little advance planning or counseling to determine what is actually involved in marriage. As a result, there is a lack of commitment. If a spouse doesn't like marriage he or she just walks away from it. There is little accountability. No wonder that, in our "quick fix" society, a growing number of marriages in America end in divorce.

3. *Rearing children* — the adolescent years — is a major crisis point for parents. Why? It's the same predictable pattern. Parents don't anticipate the issues that must be faced and do very little, if any, planning. Mothers and fathers don't educate themselves to lead their children through critical stages of development. Signals and warnings go unheeded and the children's adolescence overtakes the parents. Only after the problems start do parents start reading the "how-to-raise-teenagers" books or go to child psychologists for help.

Tragically, parents never do anything to get smart about the predictable issues of adolescence. Instead, parents fight. They fight changes happening within their children. They fight the changes happening to themselves because of their children. They fight with their spouse while deciding how to deal with the situation. And most seriously of all, they fight their children. The unfortunate consequences can include alcoholism, drug abuse, teen-age pregnancy, juvenile delinquency, and suicides. Why do teen-agers suffer from low self-esteem? The answer lies largely within parents' shortcomings.

4. With the American population graying rapidly, *retirement* has

become a growing crisis point. It doesn't have to be. Unfortunately, many people don't plan for retirement far enough in advance. They aren't prepared, emotionally or financially, for this critical period.

During the last twenty years, I have attended or presided over many retirement ceremonies. One thing I always do during the festivities is look into the eyes of the person being honored to get a reading on how he feels toward this monumental event in his life. Unfortunately, far too many have the same hollow, empty look.

I often wonder if they have reflected on their career, perhaps with a keen sense of disappointment at what they have done or not done. Do they really feel a sense of accomplishment? Have they utilized their talents and abilities wisely? Have they lived and worked near the peak of their potential, or have they wasted themselves?

For some of these retirees, forty years of work has been a millstone of existence rather than a series of milestones of personal growth. What is the reason? Many have let their careers happen to them. They didn't take charge. Now retirement becomes a crisis point.

LEARNING FROM CRISIS POINTS

Whether it's a job, marriage, raising children, moving through the work years, or facing retirement, too many people dig a hole for themselves by not developing a better understanding of the issues involved. They assume life is a continuous path upon which one foot plods along in front of the other on a steady course, and things somehow work out. They assume somebody will make good decisions on their behalf.

Most people believe divorce, adolescent tragedies, being fired, personal unhappiness, alcoholism, poor health or worse, all happen to someone else. They assume these crises won't happen to them or their loved ones. And more seriously, when problems do start happening, instead of confronting them head-on they deny that the problems exist until it's too late.

Too many people have one fundamental flaw: They don't think! They don't plan or educate themselves about these crucial times. They can't confront problems, and they deny the existence of crisis points. Instead, they just let these predictable career stages happen rather than take the steps required to minimize risks by anticipating problems and dealing with them. They need to make these predictable experiences work for them. Life would be much more rewarding, exciting, and cheerful for them if they would plan ahead.

BACK TO MID-LIFE

While I am certainly not an expert on all crisis points, I do know about mid-life. Because most books and articles hammer home the message that everyone can expect to have a time of crisis, the prediction becomes a self-fulfilling prophecy for many people. It does not have to be that way. The key is to be in control, to think ahead, to anticipate the signs. Take charge through planning, and by courageous actions head any mid-life miseries off at the pass.

If you will take some time out of life's routine and educate yourself a little, you could deal with these issues far better than most do. But the sword of Damocles for you will likely be the difficulty of knowing that the problem must be addressed, but not quite knowing what to do. So you postpone action, planning to get to it tomorrow. But tomorrow somehow never comes. You do nothing and aren't ready. At that point you are in crisis.

EXPERIENCING A NEW JOURNEY

There is mounting evidence that during mid-career years, many people experience what Gerald O'Collins describes as a period of "new spiritual awareness." For those who are receptive, this "can be a time of revelation, when new vistas open themselves to the human spirit."[7]

According to O'Collins, this reawakening inside one's self occurs after the individual embarks on a career or business venture, actively experiences "hands on" what life is all about, and becomes firmly established in the world.

The span of human life has been characterized by O'Collins as being in three broad stages: "First is the journey from childhood into maturity; second is the middle course that all persons must pass through, a journey that commences when the power of youth is gone, when the possibility of failure first presents itself and when the decisions of earlier years turn up to be shallow and pointless. The third and last journey is the trip through old age into death."

An important distinction must be made. Some people are forced into new career courses or sudden job changes due to circumstances beyond their control: For example, adverse economic conditions due to inflation or recession, industry-level difficulties (such as the collapse of oil prices, dramatic slowdown of housing markets, or demise of firms), impact of technological breakthroughs on job skills, merger mania, small business failure, public policy (decisions at the federal government level), or other drastic unforeseen changes can force job changes. Personal reasons for change include catastrophic illness, death of a relative, divorce, or the bombshell of other unexpected family circumstances.

These situations become stressful. Because some people can't handle uncertainty, decisions are often made quickly and without much reflection or introspection. Distress signals go out. A new job is found as soon as possible. Having a job, not necessarily one with quality and potential, is the goal. Adjustments are made, things settle down, and one's lifestyle is rearranged to meet different work schedules or accommodate reduced financial means. Life goes on for these individuals. The new journey for these people is short. The destination may or may not be a good one. Opportunity for careful examination of one's self, in relation to life's alternatives, is foregone in the desire to re-establish quickly a sense of personal equilibrium and family stability.

But others in mid-life experience a profound, life-changing spiritual upheaval. As described by a variety of studies, e.g., Gail Sheehy in *Passages*, it can happen like this: People find themselves well on their way to success. They have been measuring achievement by their peers' yardsticks of performance, such as title, salary, responsibility, prestige, and power. Suddenly these people feel a sense of stagnation and boredom. Existing responsibilities at work, in the community, or at home may seem to lose their importance. Restlessness sets in. Their jobs become meaningless. No longer fascinated with their career or bound to their workplace associates, people going through this transformation aren't content with past achievements or satisfied with current employment choices.

Fear of failure in life, coupled with uncertainty about the future, begins to enter their thoughts. Priorities change as life goes through various physiological stages. Those facing this dilemma begin to ask deep philosophical questions of themselves: *What am I doing? Why am I here? Is it all worth it? Am I where I want to be? Do I really need to be here? Does anybody really care? Even if they do, does it matter that much to me? Should I be some place else? How do I get there? What is happening?*

One difference between people experiencing mid-life as a positive new journey versus those experiencing a negative crisis is in the approach taken in how these questions are answered and how the dilemma is resolved. The secret is in coming to grips honestly and realistically with these feelings, and then in making tough decisions about mid-life through careful examination, personal planning, and self-management.

WHERE DO YOU FIT?

The fact is that if you are in mid-life, you have the opportunity to experience a natural, wholesome phenomenon. It should be consoling to know that you are neither crazy nor alone in your dilemma. Thousands of people every year share the same experience.

Recognize that "mid-life" is actually happening to you and then deal with it early. If a mid-life journey is beckoning, do not ignore it or assume it will go away. Instead, answer the call and manage the opportunity.

Keep in mind, as O'Collins points out, a real second journey "happens" to a person. One does not voluntarily enter into it. You can't decide to buy a ticket and take the trip. According to O'Collins, one feature of these journeys emerges clearly. Whether the causes are apparent or less obvious, "seemingly of their own volition, second journeys simply begin." But the final destination is determined by the traveler. If you are on the journey, make sure you make the effort to select the right destination. To do this, you need a road map—a game plan.

Recognize the symptoms and assess how you approach the solution. Do you stop and carefully assess what is going on in your life? Do you say, "Let me take this opportunity for a comprehensive appraisal of all aspects of myself before I make decisions about where to go from here?" Or do you yell "Mayday," leap to conclusions, and take superficial courses of action because of fear of the unknown, or pressure from peers or loved ones.

Remember, this is a major life-changing decision process. It deserves your careful attention. Ask yourself whether you have an overwhelming need for structure and clarity in life. If so, confront your dilemma and take the steps needed to be at peace with yourself. Don't play games with your life or your loved ones. This important hurdle must be overcome to experience fully the benefits of the journey.

HOW TO GET STARTED

My advice is that when the opportunity for a mid-life journey or threat of mid-life crisis presents itself, face the situation as an opportunity, not as something to be denied, ashamed of, or swept under a rug. Doing this is mostly a state of mind and attitude. Take the trip openly. Do not fight the instincts and inner feelings that are boiling over; instead, harness them and see the experience as a time of exciting discovery. While this period will be a time of tension, confusion, and uncertainty, recognizing it for what it is and addressing it honestly and positively will open new doors for personal growth, renewal of purpose, spiritual development, and inner fulfillment. But there also is an enormous cost involved.

Be prepared to pay the price, because, as O'Collins warns, taking the journey to its fullest may also close many doors to the past. Old associations will likely be terminated and you will probably cut ties with old relationships. Many times, though, this is for the better. I have found from my own experience that many of these social or workplace contacts weren't really as genuine or as important to me as I originally thought. They were valuable only because we had a mutual need for each other due to our work or civic project. You will experience the same reaction. The important point is that after reaching your new destination, you end up being a much stronger person—more independent, self-assured, refreshed, and goal-oriented.

As you take the journey, let me urge you to draw fully on your religious convictions to guide you. With this support, as you make difficult decisions and chart new careers, nothing that matters very much can hurt you. This is the beauty of faith. If you deal with this experience in a positive, forthright way, a wonderful new world awaits you.

THE MISTAKES PEOPLE MAKE

Unfortunately, most people who experience mid-life transformation never fully understand what is happening. They don't recognize the signals and by themselves can't establish a fresh sense of direction. They either get no advice or bad advice. Most depend on their own knowledge (or lack of it). Their own view of the world about them is too narrow and restricted to be helpful; therefore, they never become fully aware that they could take a healthy step, one which could open new doors of personal opportunity and spiritual fulfillment.

Instead, deeply concerned about this new ambiguity in their lives, motivated by the need for structure and routine, and influenced by desire for acceptance by peers and social groups, individuals quickly seek a permanent solution to their dilemma. As a result, they often make hasty decisions, moving aimlessly from job to job. They end up never fully addressing the spiritual questions within themselves. Instead, they compound the misery and the restlessness continues. The results include spouse or child abuse, divorce, loss of position or business, chemical dependence, or worse.

OUT OF THE CLOSET

The term "mid-life crisis" is negative and inappropriate. The use of this label does a great disservice to an enormous number of people who need to understand better, from a positive perspective, the emotional forces at work in their lives. Mid-life is a second journey which should be brought out into the sunshine so it can be fully understood and appreciated.

Since the second journey is both normal and predictable, it should be treated as such. Self-appraisals at mid-life are not just the result of emotional instability or failure in one's life. Therefore, second-journey experiences need to be dealt with in a positive, career-guiding way.

If you think this mid-life phenomenon is happening to you, do not deny it, be embarrassed by it, ignore it, cast it aside, or fight it. Instead, see it as a fresh opportunity. Nurture and explore what it means for you. Seek professional guidance from respected sources early. Study literature now available on the subject. Based on respected advice from qualified professionals, face the symptoms squarely and maturely. Be self-disciplined throughout the entire discovery process. Bring spouse and family into the analysis early. Take charge and stay in control. Search for the satisfaction and fulfillment that can come.

REMEMBER THE MESSAGE

The good news is that many people have successfully undergone profound changes in their middle years and have led deeply enriched and more promising lives as a result. Therefore, the goal of a mid-life journey should be the expansion of one's potential into life's uncharted areas. This experience awaits those willing to unshackle the past, those who have a pioneer spirit, those who possess the courage to risk over-turning life's routine, and those who can defy the conventional wisdom and pressure from peers.

Best wishes if you are embarking on a new journey in your life. Be patient as you seek new meaning. Grab the reins and stay in the driver's seat. Draw on all the resources available deep within you. Especially seek God's help at this crucial time in your career. Stretch your potential as a person and spiritual being to the fullest. You will be glad you did.

SECOND JOURNEY CHECKLIST

- Be aware that "second journeys" are to be expected as a normal process of life.
- Use your "second journey" as an opportunity for growth and happiness.
- Remember that you are not alone. Others have successfully made the "second journey" transition. If you know some of these people, share with them—and listen!

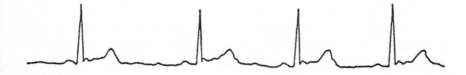

11

WHAT IF YOU LIVE
TO BE A HUNDRED?

Treat 75 as if it were the speed limit, not your age.
— Lady Bird Johnson, on the occasion of her 75th birthday

Does it sound far-fetched that you or anyone else could reasonably expect to live 100 years? Not on your life. If you were born since 1946, the odds are one in three that you will live to age 85. One million baby boomers—Americans born between 1946 and 1964—will live to be 100. What's happening?[8]

The answer is that our society is aging dramatically. Even though we think of ourselves as a young nation, with all the emphasis in advertising and in the workplace on youth, a "revolution in longevity is taking place in this country that is changing our lives," according to a recently published article based on the 1986 study, "Our Aging Society: Paradox and Promise."[9]

Demographers put the finger on a "combination of low fertility rates (in the post-baby boom years), a lower mortality rate, and increased longevity."

Think about all the implications of living ten decades with good physical health and mental alertness. If you lived this long, as more and more Americans will, how would you spend every season of your life? Every year, every month, every week, every day, every hour, every minute? Would your time be spent productively? With enjoyment?

With satisfaction? And, most importantly to this book, what would be the implications to your career?

As a beginning, you would outlive your current place of employment regardless of how you felt about working there. Why? Businesses change. Industries change. Technologies change. Economics change. Most of these changes are beyond your ability to control. What you must do is prepare for them and respond in areas—personal interests, needs, priorities—over which you have control. Don't let retirement sneak up on you and become an albatross of empty time and empty pockets. This is the importance of career planning.

WHAT ARE THE IMPLICATIONS OF EXTENDED LIFE?

1. Even in the best of circumstances, you would likely hold many jobs and have several careers throughout your work life. Employment instability, job mobility, skills upgrading, and starting over would become the norm.

2. Individuals, employers, insurance companies, and governments will have to rethink retirement age, employee health plans, financial security programs, and pension payment options. It is obvious that Social Security will not be a sound cornerstone of personal retirement planning. Mental and physical well-being will become increasingly important issues for those facing 25 or more years of life after retirement.

3. As is already happening, traditionally family-oriented women will be re-educated, re-equipped with marketable skills, and presented with time utilization challenges required for a full life after the children have left the nest. This is true even if the kids return home for the second or third time—after college, after jobs, and often after divorce. Remember, we are talking about having 40 to 50 years of useful life after the children are gone.

4. Education will be a lifelong process, not only training for skills needed to survive in the workplace, but for hobby and avocational interests required to stay mentally alert and challenged. This is good because it means life won't be a millstone of unhappiness, boredom, and frustration.

How could such a thing happen? The average life span of Americans is creeping up, now reaching 75 or 80 years. The federal government recently predicted that the life expectancy of newborns is now nearly 75 years, but those who have already reached 75 years should add another 11 years to expected life. That's 86 years! With additional scientific discoveries and lifestyle changes, projections will go even higher and higher each year. Today there are at least 26,000 Americans who are 100 or more years old. The number will grow rapidly, reaching 100,000 by the year 2000, then swelling to 400,000 by 2025 and to one million in 2050.

There are four basic reasons for increased life expectancy. The first is high-tech medicine, such as breakthroughs in research on the main killers—heart disease and cancer. Fitness is the second reason. This includes better attention to the care and feeding of our bodies. The third reason is more education and regulations dealing with health hazards, smoking, and other bodily abuses. The fourth reason has to do with safety. We are more aware of safety and accident prevention on highways, on the job, and in the home.

Health care and medical technology is creating miracle after miracle, and the best is yet to come if we can afford the cost. We have only seen the tip of the iceberg of biotechnology. Such things as cancer cures, brain cell regeneration, arm and leg muscle pacemakers, and cryobiology-based organ transplants will become commonplace. The impressive list goes on and on.

PAYOFF OF TAX DOLLARS

From where do all the high-tech medical breakthroughs come? Part of the answer is from aerospace programs! We sometimes lose sight of the tremendous influence on our lives of space research and development. Billions of dollars pumped into space programs during the last 30 years are bearing much fruit for the benefit of mankind far beyond satellites and moon walks.

Since the Mercury, Gemini, Apollo, and space shuttle programs, laboratory technology has developed at blinding speed. Transfers of sophisticated technology to the medical field are creating applications for better health and longer life. They are coming faster than delivery systems can absorb or put them to practical use at a price the health-care marketplace can afford.

SOME THINGS TO THINK ABOUT

Sophisticated mechanisms are already in place to support dramatic increases in life expectancy and healthy aging! What if you lived to be a strong and alert 100 years old, with the potential of enjoying a productive life the entire time? Quality of life— not age—is the central issue. What would you do with your time? How would you remain intellectually challenged and mentally excited? Would you be prepared financially to live 20 or 30 years beyond retirement? Could you afford a lifestyle of dignity with your pension income and other resources?

Does the possibility of living this long sound preposterous? Put it into perspective. Did you think man could ever travel to the moon? And what about the impact of transistors, the atom, lasers, vaccines, microchips, fiber optics, superconductors, and high-tech appliances we have surrounded ourselves with? Increasingly, the future we daydream about is becoming reality in our everyday lives.

EXPLODING THE MYTHS OF AGING

An increasing number of workers are electing to retire prematurely or are being forced into taking early retirement. Some are entering retirement during their fifties.

If you are considering early retirement—whether by choice or by order—and its sometimes less demanding lifestyle, consider the following points raised by Alan Pifer and D. Lydia Bronte.[10] You may change your mind.

1. Medical achievements and health awareness have changed the relationship of the term "old" and age 60 established in the 1930's, when Social Security legislation was drafted.

2. The idea of age 65 as the crucial point of mandatory retirement in workplaces everywhere has been effectively eliminated.

3. Physical old age, which once began as early as age 55 or 60, has been postponed for most people to age 75, 80, or 90, due to what is known as "healthy aging."

4. Researchers are coining a new phrase for the concept of long life: "The Third Quarter of Life." This term refers to a period in which

people are still fully engaged in life and have too much vigor and energy to withdraw from the satisfaction of their work and regular activities.

5. Neither the term "middle age" nor that of "old age" fits this stage of life—roughly between the ages of 50 and 75.

6. Many people in their fifties have financial commitments—such as a college education for their children, mortgages, and other financial obligations. A pension or another form of fixed income will likely be insufficient to meet the payments.

This new concept of longevity means that those entering the "third quarter" have roughly half of their lives still before them, possibly up to 50 years or more.

The implications of an aging society on retirement, personal productivity, and human dignity are quickly closing in on us.

7. People by the thousands are going to the sidelines at the peak of their productivity and usefulness in the workplace.

8. Society grossly underestimates the strength and potential of people in these added years of life. Understandably, then, there are few avenues for people in this age range to channel their vitality and creativity. Their personal growth is stifled.

9. Career counselors and institutional mechanisms for guiding and financing "third quarter" career changes are non-existent at this point.

10. Existing hiring practices and employer attitudes generally work against the older worker. In fact, the more experienced a worker becomes, the more negative the corporate attitude grows. Younger managers are in charge, without an appreciation of the value and potential contribution to be made by older workers.

DON'T MAKE RETIREMENT A WAKE

Retiring with a quarter of a century of useful time remaining and aging with dignity raise extremely tough questions. They are frightening and mind-boggling. These matters must be dealt with individually and at local, state, and federal levels as public policy issues. In the meantime, the consequences to you of not honestly and openly facing the question of aging as it will affect you personally will be extremely tragic.

When coping with this delicate topic for yourself, or perhaps on behalf of older members of your family, follow the central theme of this book. Do not assume somebody else is worrying about your post-retirement years for you. Do not depend on government, employer, or family to provide for your economic and emotional well-being in the later years. Do something now to secure the financial security and quality of your retirement. Go over this book very carefully and reflect on the self-management concepts. Put them to work.

Based on the information throughout this book, answer some vital questions about aging. Do you need a personal career and financial plan for every stage and age of your life? Are you really ready for retirement? Are you willing to pay the price, perhaps giving up current pleasures, to finance your post-retirement plan?

It's decision time. Come to grips with these issues. Contact your local or state commission on aging. Learn as much as possible about aging and the changing demographics in this country, then make responsible decisions for your future.

AGING WITH DIGNITY

The need for a strategic plan to manage your career to the fullest becomes increasingly important when it's put in the context of the remaining years of life. You need to deal with retirement, in advance, while you can. Answer these questions: *How many post-retirement years could I have? What are the potential productive uses of my time in retirement? What personal preparations will be required of me now to be ready to enjoy a long life? What will happen to me if I don't make plans and let retirement happen to me? What should I do next?*

LIVING TO A HUNDRED CHECKLIST

- Rethink the "script" about the future. What are the personal implications of your living to be 100 in terms of your continuing education, your financial planning, and your new career options?
- Consider the problems that could emerge if you outlive your personal resources. What plans should you make now?

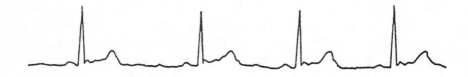

12

GAME PLAN FOR THOSE NOW "IN BETWEEN JOBS"

It is ironic that thousands of bosses have been shocked to discover that the one thing they weren't prepared for was their own firing. Many are now botching their job hunting efforts.

Thousands of workers are being furloughed indefinitely, laid off permanently, retired prematurely, or fired outright for reasons beyond their control. Headlines feature job loss statistics that mark a personal catastrophe for more and more Americans. In nuclear age terminology, people are experiencing "job meltdown."

The technological renaissance sweeping our land, coupled with increased economic pressure on U.S. industry to compete more effectively in the world's marketplace, is taking a heavy toll on white collar and blue collar employees alike.

Careers are being disrupted. Families are being uprooted. Dreams are being postponed. Retirement plans are being shattered. Unfortunately, most people facing sudden loss of job are being caught by surprise. With no inkling that this could happen, the majority are suddenly unemployed without good options readily available. Very few are using a definite, preplanned strategy for dealing with job hunting in a rational way.

If unexpected loss of job has happened to you due to reasons beyond your control, or if you have been fired because of your own doing, it is time to be decisive and demonstrate personal leadership. Take charge of your own future. To do this effectively you need a plan.

But first, clear the air. This is no time to feel sorry for yourself, to go "off the deep end," or to toss in the towel emotionally. Instead, it's the precise moment to regroup. I urge you to press on with renewed hope and optimism for the future. Turn this problem into an opportunity. Base this on confidence in yourself, by having a self-developed plan of action and by drawing on faith in a Higher Being.

BUILDING A FRESH BEGINNING

The following 36 ideas provide a framework to help you develop a strategy for getting your act together, finding new employment, and establishing a new career.

1. Don't panic! Control your anger and bitterness. Get over any feelings of devastation. Don't take it personally if losing your job was not your fault.

Belaboring reasons for your termination won't help. Rehashing or dwelling on it will sap valuable energy and will drain your spirit. You will need to draw heavily on both.

2. If losing your job was your fault, whatever the reason, admit it to yourself and to your family. Then put the matter behind you. Do not dwell on failure or past mistakes. Do not consider yourself a failure. Do not make excuses or blame others. Do not kick the cat and vent your frustration on your loved ones. Instead, come to grips with the reality of your plight. Close the door to this unfortunate chapter of your life. Learn from the experience and move ahead. In short, begin now to become a better person as a result of what happened and just get on with life.

3. Whatever the circumstances of your termination, develop a fresh start attitude. Take the position that there are new worlds to conquer and now is the right time to start. Listen to inspirational tapes and read motivational books to clear the mind and get the positive juices flowing.

4. Establish a four-part game plan and get going in your job search. Your top priority should be to take care of yourself and your family on these crucial points:

- Financial well-being

- Mental well-being
- Physical well-being
- Spiritual well-being

5. Said another way, as you begin your journey to new employment, take the necessary steps to protect your reputation, your credit, your appearance, your health, and your sanity.

6. To get started, lean on your loved ones for support and encouragement. It will strengthen them as well. If you don't have a support group, find one. I cannot emphasize this point enough. Do not try to carry all your emotional burdens alone. You need to have a few people whom you know and trust to confide in. Examples are: neighbors, close friends, Sunday school class, golf or bowling buddies, and family. They can help you deal with feelings of loneliness and renew your sense of self-confidence.

7. Find a friend who can be your confidant. If you're married, it may be your spouse. Or it may not be, depending on how much that person can uplift and support your battered ego. It's often better to find a friend who will be willing to listen—that takes the stress off the marriage relationship and lets you focus on your quality time with your spouse. Bare your burdens with this friend. Don't ask him to assume the load, but expect him to be honest with you. Accept his thoughts, ideas, and suggestions, but make your own decisions. A friend can be the best outlet valve you have so you can redirect your energies in a positive fashion. The important thing is to realize that you are still the same person you were before you were fired or laid off. The only thing that has changed is your employment status.

8. Operate on the assumption that it could take from six months to a year to find suitable work, depending on the economy, the market for your specific skills, and your mobility. It is crucial that you take an accurate reading of your current circumstances. Carefully review your financial situation. List your basic cash flow requirements for food, utilities, mortgage payments, insurance, and other fixed installment commitments. Determine any net severance arrangement, and how it will be paid. Ask yourself: How large is my rainy day fund? What other sources of income or cash flow do I have to carry me through my job search?

9. In the absence of adequate savings and cash flow to meet your current level of living, bite the bullet now. Freeze all unnecessary spending immediately. Cut your standard of living to the bone. Reduce your

lifestyle to a bare maintenance level. Examine your household budget. If necessary, restructure monthly payments. Collect all credit cards and lock them up. Go strictly to a cash basis. Gear your spending to a survival strategy. Eat more pasta and less steak. *Focus on saving money rather than saving face.*

10. Practice an "Up and Out" routine every day. Stay on your normal sleeping schedule. Get moving and get out of the house at your regular time. Do not sit around and mope. If possible, find a place to set up shop while looking for work. Set goals to accomplish something every day. Spend every waking hour planning and implementing the job-seeking strategy you develop. Leave no stone unturned.

11. Exercise regularly. Mental, physical, and emotional health come with exercise. If you haven't been working out under a controlled plan, start now. A good aerobic routine will calm your nerves, reduce stress, and make you feel better. Exercise also gives you a good chance to think. Keep yourself refreshed. Don't become stale.

12. Read books on self-analysis, resumé preparation, job hunting strategies, what works and doesn't work in today's job market, and on coping eventually with life's transitions. These materials can be found in most bookstores.

13. It is important to use these resources (books and tapes) to help sharpen your ability to sell yourself. Clearly define your job objectives. Communicate these objectives and what you have to offer prospective employers. Market your unique skills and proven abilities in an increasingly competitive workplace.

14. At this point you face a moment of truth. It is at this precise time in your business or professional career that you learn firsthand who your friends are and to whom you can turn for help. There is an ancient proverb which goes like this. *"Wealth has many friends, but a man without means loses the friend he has."* Your present circumstances will test this theory.

15. Do not depend on any of these relationships to find you a new job. Don't sit by the phone passively waiting for their help. You will probably find that most of your business-oriented contacts end up being of little value to you. The raw truth is that most business relationships have an "out of sight, out of mind" attitude about you and your problems. When you are out of their sight, you are also out of their mind. Don't be offended. This is predictable and expected. Most of your former colleagues and associates have their own concerns to worry

about. Unfortunately, these are the facts of life in today's increasingly tough, impersonal, and unstable workplace.

Whom Can You Count On?

Type of Relationships	*You Have*	*Help in Finding a Job*
Company Colleagues	Many	Practically zero
Professional Acquaintances	Several	Very little
Close Business Associates	A few	Some—maybe
True Personal Friends	One or two	As much as possible

16. If you have a network of contacts and relationships, put it to work for you. This includes former associates, family, friends, university placement offices, and others with current information about the job market. Keep your network alive by making contacts regularly but without wearing it thin. This requires judgment on your part. Most networks are fragile at best. Quite frankly, most are really more form than substance anyway. But networking is in vogue and is something you are supposed to do, so keep at it. You might get a useful lead.

17. You will also discover that lunches with professional acquaintances, former company colleagues, and others on your network list will play out quickly. Phone calls will be returned less and less frequently. As time passes you will be more and more alone in your job search. At some point, you will probably feel a loss of connectiveness because you have been removed from your past work life. This is why family and support groups are vital as a source of enduring strength and encouragement.

18. Do not count on people who made money off you in your former job. Vendors of goods and services who successfully courted you while you were of value to them will be of little help now. Include in this group your contacts in advertising and public relations agencies, insurance agents, bankers, accountants, lawyers, other professionals, as well as most vendors of supplies and materials. They will be too busy soliciting the business of your successors to spend much time on your behalf.

19. If you have been provided the services of an outplacement firm, use it, but don't sit idle and depend on your outplacement representative

to do your work for you. The decision to use these organizations is usually to soothe the conscience of your former employer. Helping you get a new job is largely a by-product. These organizations will generate a lot of activity on your behalf. Sometimes, there is more smoke than fire in terms of solid leads and successful contacts. This will depend on the quality of the specific outplacement firm selected. While most outplacement firms have good features, particularly in career counseling and redirection, put this source of job hunting assistance on your list as just one alternative.

20. Registering with an employment agency may be okay if you are satisfied that they have expertise in job areas of interest to you. Understand that, unless you pay a fee, employment agencies always represent the employer, not you. Employment agencies typically have very limited coverage of the job market and usually only have access to lower level jobs.

21. There is growing evidence that sending unsolicited resumés is not a very productive approach to job hunting. Organizations are typically inundated with resumés and employment applications. These are generally filed away or just tossed out. The secret is timing and getting someone's attention. Most resumés are poorly written anyway and should not even be used. A well-phrased introductory letter may be a better attention getter.

22. Your chances of finding new managerial-level employment through an executive search firm ("head hunter") are also extremely slim. Making contact, getting on the circuit, and striking a deal through this means is tough. But in the spirit of leaving no stone unturned, try anyway. You might be the exception.

23. By the way, who are you anyway? Perhaps you are going about your job hunt the wrong way. It is time to stop and take a careful look at yourself. What do you stand for? Do you really know yourself? Evaluate your goals and priorities. Do they really make sense? Assess your psychological needs and interests. Undergo a comprehensive career planning evaluation by someone professionally qualified but with absolutely no financial stake in finding your next job. Why is this important?

24. You may discover you have been asking yourself the wrong questions and have been going in the wrong direction. This is especially important if you are focusing your search in your comfort zone: locating a job in a similar industry. In fact, you might just be missing an un-

usual opportunity. Maybe you need to step back and ask more penetrating questions. Perhaps you should be thinking about changing careers rather than just thinking about a job shift. The secret to your future might be in finding an entirely new direction with new purpose. Perhaps it's time to take a 180 degree turn in your career and life.

25. Is there anything else, substantially different, that you have ever thought about trying? If you feel locked in by organizational bureaucracies, stifled by corporate cultures, and hamstrung by company rules or rituals, maybe it's time to explore new horizons.

26. If you have a gray flannel suit mentality, and for all practical purposes have been a corporate "yes" person, perhaps it is time to explore your entrepreneurial instincts. Probe honestly to see if you really have what it takes to become independent and be your own boss (review the information contained in Chapter 13).

27. There may be an even deeper contributing cause for the circumstances you are in. Perhaps the reasons leading up to the job hunting dilemma you are experiencing are being influenced by forces working deep within you. There is the strong possibility that a new person is evolving, with new interests and new values. Your real problem may be an internal identity crisis. This phenomenon happens to many people on life's journey. Unfortunately, few people recognize the changes as they are taking place, and even fewer ever come to grips with them. The best way to describe this set of circumstances is the so-called "mid-life crisis." Chapter Ten deals with this topic in more detail.

28. The best advice is to accept your present circumstances as a time of discovery. You may very well be at the greatest moment of opportunity of your life. Your so-called misfortune may instead be a threshold for refreshing and exciting new growth. With the right attitude and support from those who depend upon you, the chance to explore new avenues for career fulfillment and personal happiness may be at hand.

29. It may be very difficult for you to accept this possibility or to think clearly about all the ramifications of taking a dramatic turn in your career path. Since life is full of uncertainty right now you are perhaps experiencing sharp cuts in income and adjustment in lifestyle, coupled with anxiety about your future. You may feel intense pressure to land a job quickly.

30. Whatever your situation, please do not overlook this possibility of mid-life restlessness or take this opportunity for new career direction

lightly. Be creative and imaginative in your thinking. Brainstorm! Don't think "job"—think "career." Expand your horizons. Think new and fresh thoughts about your skills and job interests. Can you transfer your abilities and experiences to new areas of employment? As a beginning, think beyond what you have done narrowly as an occupation for all these years to what else is out there as a career opportunity. Broaden your view of the world. Escape the clutches of your peers and seek advice from a variety of non-traditional sources. Look for the upside challenges and downside risks of new possibilities.

31. An important hurdle to overcome in developing a new sense of direction comes from yourself. Too often, people measure success solely in terms of title, power, possessions, and income. This lets ego get in the way of reason and limits your thinking. If you suffer from this malady, but are willing to change your yardstick of achievement, you could discover there are many new worlds to conquer. Many people have come to grips with having less money and less cosmetic lifestyle while finding much more personal challenge and inner fulfillment.

32. If you are licking your wounds and nursing a bruised ego because of a sudden loss of authority and power, I have more bad news for you. Most people in your former place of employment couldn't care less who you are or that you have departed. The truth is that most people around you—your former associates and subordinates—envied your authority and coveted your power. The focus was on the office you held rather than the person filling the job—you. In fact, eighty percent of the people back at the office couldn't care less that you are gone. Another 15 percent are glad you bit the dust, and perhaps no more than five percent have any feeling of empathy for you at all. Keep in mind that, fairly or unfairly, any problems your organization was having at the time of your departure have been shifted by the survivors to your account.

33. The measure of success that really matters is what you are as a person and what you stand for. Especially important are how you value people who were lower than you in your organization and those outside your place of employment. How do you relate to people? Are you sensitive to people's needs? Also, are you supportive of other people's opportunities? Were you a mentor or a good role model for younger people? What really counts as you develop your career are your basic values, your causes, the philosophical issues you support, and the moral and ethical stands you take. Keep in mind always that people who work with you or for you know you for "what you are." Awareness of this basic

principle should drive your behavior as a worker, manager, or professional.

34. Be careful not to confuse envy with respect. People with power and position may be envied but are not necessarily respected. Which quality is more important to a person's life? This is the acid test. As you chart your future course, which do you seek? Maybe you need to think about priorities. Don't let desire for power and need for authority become stumbling blocks to genuine career fulfillment and personal happiness. It is vital that life be a spiritual journey rather than an ego trip. This is a matter of maturity versus insecurity that needs to be worked out.

35. Be realistic! While exploring new ideas about yourself, it is obviously a matter of great importance that you keep your attention focused on your strategy for returning to the ranks of the employed. This is particularly true if you are strapped for funds and do not have the financial means to spend much time in a job search. In the final analysis, be brutally honest with yourself about strengths and weaknesses. You have to possess something somebody "has to have" and market it. If you can't make some money for someone or make a contribution to their goals, why do they need you? Understand your skills, aptitudes, flexibility, and marketability. Know your limits.

36. Never forget that individual performance in America's workplace is generally determined by one's abilities and motivation working together. The workplace demands that you deliver them both to the very best of your ability. When you do this, you will get luckier and luckier as you seek continued career growth and achievement.

SPECIAL MESSAGE FOR SPOUSES

Be aware of the "flying solo" trap. A phenomenon often experienced by people facing career shock is *"aloneness"* as in: "I can deal with this problem by myself," or "It's my problem and no one else's," or "I must protect my family from seeing my uncertainty, confusion, and frustration because they won't know how to handle it." This attitude results in only one thing—a desperate feeling that gets in the way of finding new employment.

As the mate of a person who is experiencing employment turbulence, either through job loss, job insecurity, or a dead end, it is important that you determine if aloneness has set in. Let your spouse know that he or she has a source of strength, security, and fellowship at the breakfast table each morning. Express your support often and in various positive ways—in words and by actions. Ongoing communications designed to minimize the "flying solo" syndrome is critical.

People who have faced job turbulence tell me that they literally would have gone off the deep end without a spouse's encouragement, support, and continued love. Yet these serious job setbacks don't affect just the emotions of the employee: They spread to other family members whose source of stability in life is bounded by the bread winner's income, insurance, and regular employment. It extends to the children who aren't sure why dad or mom is suddenly now at home or why life's routine has abruptly changed.

If you have a spouse who is experiencing job-related trauma, it's important that you understand what emotional issues are involved. If there are children, they need to know that your spouse may hit the pits emotionally. Whatever the prevailing attitude or behavior during these rocky times, family members of all ages need to know that they are still loved. You must prevent their emotional world from being turned upside down by this situation. This is a tough assignment.

HOW YOU CAN HELP

Here are 14 suggestions for understanding your spouse's dilemma and for providing assistance during the job turbulence experience:

1. Job loss is as demeaning an experience as a person can endure. No longer is there a strong sense of purpose, a drive to get up and go, or a boss to whom to be responsible. Job loss can be emotionally crippling unless it's addressed quickly and dealt with positively. A plan of action is needed to give a sense of direction and hope.

2. The last thing a person who has faced layoff, job termination or other job-related trauma needs is continued castigation over whose fault it is. Chances are good that the fault could be placed with several different persons or factors. Anyway, what is to be gained by rubbing salt in the wounds at this point?

3. Don't nag. Questions or comments such as "Why aren't you out trying to find a job?" or "You lost the job again?" or "What are we going to do now?" do nothing to help. Instead, these barbs drive your spouse

further and further into a mental shell, making it more difficult to maintain a positive attitude and be attractive to prospective employers.

4. Be a cheerleader, confidante, and supporter. Create an atmosphere that the home is a "safe harbor" from the perils of the job market.

5. While job loss is painful for all parties, it doesn't have to result in complete departure from normal family relations and, in particular, normal marital relationships. Being a loving spouse—yes, even more sexually romantic—will make the difference in how a person feels about himself or herself. This translates into how your spouse attacks the job market, because when people feel good about themselves, they become more assured and self- confident.

6. None of this means you have to subliminate your own career or interests, unduly cater to your spouse, or otherwise become a martyr in the dilemma at hand, but you should do everything reasonably possible to help your mate protect his or her self- worth and self-esteem.

7. A word of caution. If both husband and wife are pursuing careers and one is achieving success while the other is experiencing a job-related crisis, it is very important that no gloating occur. Do not "rub it in" with too much conversation, perhaps well-intended, about all the good things happening to you. Play it cool and be humble. Play down your achievements. Focus your attention on helping your spouse recover and get going again.

8. Encourage your spouse to maintain some regularity in life. Become familar with the content of this chapter and encourage him or her to develop a strategy for spending regular hours of resumé writing, phone calling, cold calling, and other aspects of the job search. Be positive in the way you come across.

9. On the other hand, be prepared to see your spouse ensconced in a favorite chair reading a favorite magazine or book. You've got to let a sense of timing *lead* the job search process. Pushing with the admonition "Don't come back until you get a job" could eventually lead your spouse to do just that.

10. Encourage your spouse to use this period of unemployment to spend time with the kids, with friends and yes, even with you. Also keep in mind that while children are in school, they can't interrupt quiet walks, talks over lunch, or even special times alone.

11. Become a partner in the job search. You will also have to be prepared for emotional highs and lows during this time — perhaps for months. Get to know the current line-up of prospects, the status of each,

and the game plan for following through. When an interview goes well, share the excitement. When the rejection letters arrive, don't make a special case out of it.

12. There will be times when your spouse doesn't want to deal with home problems, school problems, kid problems, neighbor problems or fix-it problems. His or her mind may be on a thousand and one things related to the job search. Because of this, your flexibility, understanding, patience, and sense of emotional timing can be a great benefit to you both.

13. If you can't deal with the emotions and strains of your spouse's unemployment or job frustrations, encourage him or her to find a responsible third party—a pastor, psychologist, friend or someone who can be a good listener. Most people are reluctant to bring an outsider into the emotional equation. This compounds the "aloneness" phenomenon discussed earlier.

Your encouragement on this point allows your loved one to vent frustrations and concerns to a neutral party, minimizing the potential for chaos at home. I've spent many an hour listening to friends vent emotions that could not be constructively expressed at home. A neutral party can become a safety valve in your own family's life. Don't underestimate the value of this suggestion.

14. Finally, whatever you do, remember the words of your marriage vows: "In sickness (unemployment) and in health (employment), for richer (with a regular paycheck coming in) or for poorer (with the unemployment check arriving weekly)," because their implications are even deeper during this time of emotional crisis.

BUT WHAT ABOUT YOU?

As a spouse, trying to be loving and supportive in a worst-of-times situation will probably be impossible until you face openly and deal honestly with your own inner feelings. Loss, shame, anger, guilt, and self-blame may each overwhelm *you* as you contemplate how to be supportive of your spouse. Consider these to be normal feelings of someone whose spouse is going through tough times.

Try to deal with these emotions head on. Anger is natural. Perhaps a friend could be your sounding board for lashing out. You may experience guilt when in reality there is no basis for it. Each of these frustrating feelings can be faced and dealt with in like manner.

There is nothing wrong with going into a closet and crying your eyes out—once or twice. In fact, letting the pressure off this way from time to time may be the best therapy going for you. But real help can best be found in a friend or acquaintance who has been there and who was able to conquer feelings such as these, going on to be a pillar of support for the spouse in crisis. Draw on their own experience and how they handled it. Have your own support group. Perhaps you need to seek out a neutral third party to help you cope with the issues you face.

The point is not to develop a martyr attitude and try to carry the burden of being a good spouse without the help of others.

LET'S REVIEW

The spouse can play a vital role in helping the mate recover from job-related trauma, particularly loss of employment. Don't make bad matters worse by unwittingly contributing to the problem of "aloneness." Instead, provide leadership in getting the matter resolved as smoothly as possible through love, support, and encouragement. The home should be a safe harbor. Remember, you're in it together ("for better or for worse"), so stick together. Be a team in sharing any aloneness while seeking a solution to the problem.

THE BALL IS IN YOUR COURT

Do you have what it takes to recover, refresh yourself, and move ahead? Or have you become stale, outdated, and perhaps even obsolete in your thinking and approaches? You need to face up to what will be required for you to regroup, retool, and press on. Do it quickly.

I wish you sincere good luck in your search for rewarding work. Maybe you will also find new meaning in your life. When you get resettled, remember to spend your paycheck wisely. Always stay within your financial means. Put some money aside now in a rainy day fund. You may be "in between" again some day. If you didn't do this financial planning the first time around it's not your fault. But next time, if you find yourself pinched financially while in-between jobs, you will have no one to blame but yourself.

CAREER CHANGE CHECKLIST

- Do something each day toward your new career.
- Maintain a positive attitude. Avoid resentment and self-pity.
- Find a support group—family or friends—to nurture you toward new goals.
- Explore all viable options. Don't just look for a job— reshape your career.

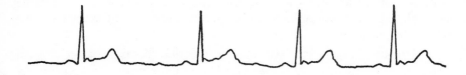

13

THE SIREN'S LURE
TO ENTREPRENEURSHIP

The good news is that new small businesses are cropping up in record numbers, creating fresh opportunity for thousands of would be entrepreneurs. The bad news is that 75 percent of these businesses will fail in five or six years.

During the past few years there has been an explosion of entrepreneurial activity in America. Small business start-ups have been unprecedented, averaging over 600,000 each year compared to 250,000 just 10 years ago and compared to about 50,000 annually in the 1950's.

People by the droves are changing careers voluntarily. They are bailing out of corporations. Statistics reflect a trend toward small business caused by a yearning for personal independence, a desire for control over one's destiny, and the need to preserve self-worth.

For thousands of executives, managers, and ordinary workers, big business as a career has lost its glitter. Corporate life can no longer provide for employees' basic needs. They want freedom! They see that corporate security is a fantasy. Small business start-ups also mirror the tremendous number of people being forced out of corporations due to massive retrenching and restructuring.

Employment forecasts for the past few years have consistently predicted that new jobs in the United States are being created at the annual rate of two to three million. Two-thirds of these jobs are in companies employing fewer than 100 people.

Ninety percent of all new jobs are in service industries with 40 percent at minimum wage levels. Seventy percent of all jobs are now service related. By the year 2000, approximately four out of every five jobs will be in the service sector.

The small business movement in America seems to be feeding on itself. The question is: Will there be enough customers to go around? How many pizza parlors, carpet cleaners, lawn services, video shops, travel agencies, and tanning salons can a community support? From where will the basic economic activity required to support these businesses come?

If you are considering investing in a small business, think about this issue very carefully. As you plan your future business venture or investment opportunity, assess the potential for profitability in specific small businesses for the next 15 or 20 years. It will be a very important consideration. The answer will not be obvious.

THE GENIUS OF AMERICA

For 200 years, entrepreneurship has been the real genius of America. It embodies the freedom of individuals to seek opportunity, the freedom to try, to excel, and to win. Our capitalistic business system gives us freedom of choice. Victor Kiam, the Remington Razor promotor, has posed the question: "Are you an entrepreneur? If you have what it takes," he says, "go for it."

Should you take his advice and answer the call to entrepreneurship? Maybe you should become your own boss as an independent spirit sweeps the country. Maybe you shouldn't. The stakes are high, and the issues are complex. Here are some common sense items to consider.

ARE YOU RUNNING FROM SOMETHING?

The very first question you should honestly and candidly answer about yourself is: Are you running from the present? Are you experiencing a mid-career plateau or late-career frustration? Are you angry or disappointed with progress in your current job? If the answer to any of these questions is yes, you are being motivated by the wrong reasons and might be making a drastic mistake.

If bailing out of where you are is your primary motive for considering a small business venture, your heart is probably not in it. Entrepreneurship requires major psychological commitment and emotional staying power. Without these qualities you can't muster the inner strength required to overcome the hardships, confinements, restrictions, discouragements, and disappointments that go with the territory.

But emotional commitment isn't enough. All the desires, motives, and good intentions you posses can never substitute for the entrepreneurial skills, managerial abilities, personality makeup, and financial requirements necessary for success. Don't delude yourself into thinking your past experience from corporations, or even technical and sales-type jobs, will transfer into the broad-based managerial skills needed to succeed in a small business. In reality, your abilities may be poles apart from the survival skills required to succeed. Owning and operating a small business is deceptively complex.

ARE YOU HEADING TOWARD SOMETHING?

On the other hand, are you running toward something—an idea, a concept, a dream? Do you have a vision and the ability to focus on that vision? If you have the right stuff in a managerial and promotional sense, are armed with sufficient money to sustain the business over the lean years, and possess the emotional qualities required, the answer is that perhaps you should start your own business. But your decision should still be a definite maybe. You must have a solid business plan based on reliable research to back up your specific idea.

SMALL BUSINESS FACTS OF LIFE

When assessing small business opportunities, keep in mind the following realities:

1. The deck is stacked against you from the beginning. Success has simply been an illusion for entirely too many people through the years. Three-fourths of all new small businesses fail within five to six years. These grim statistics have held true for the past 30 years.

2. There are four basic reasons small businesses fail: competence, customers, capital, and competition. There is usually not enough of the

first three and too much of the latter. Each of these factors must be carefully analyzed. The fundamental lessons are (1) don't get into something you don't understand and (2) don't buy into a business if you don't know how to sell or apply financial controls to it.

3. Just because a person has been highly successful in a corporate position does not mean the same individual can transfer those skills to small business. The broad management expertise required, time commitment demanded, and emotional involvement needed to make the business successful can be entirely different from one's strengths in past experiences. Wearing all the hats while doing all the worrying and most of the work, coupled with dealing with customers, suppliers, and employees all day long, and even sweeping the floor, can be a very humbling experience. Much soul searching should be done on this issue.

4. Also keep in mind that beginning a business with which you are unfamiliar, attempting to learn it from the top down at the same time, can be extremely difficult to pull off. If you are contemplating making a major investment in a business you know little about, particularly if there is a significant amount of technology or other complexities involved, think again about the amount of risk you would be taking. Too often, once committed, there is never enough time to learn all the subtle details requiring constant attention if the business is going to succeed under your management. Instead, one might be better off in the long run by first becoming an employee, working at the bottom, getting "hands on" knowledge about operating the business before you commit your financial resources.

5. Most unsuccessful small business operators kill themselves with too much optimism. They are big on startups, but weak on follow through. These people succeed for awhile, mainly on momentum, but then they fail. You can generally count on needing 50 percent more capital than you anticipated. Even under the best circumstances, you should plan on taking twice as long as you originally expected before you get rolling toward profitability and success. The key word is "sustain." Have enough of all the ingredients required to get you over the rough startup phase and allow you to gain needed experience and seasoning. Never, ever start a business on a shoestring coupled with blind faith.

6. Other qualities many small business owners lack include a sense of timing-related strategic decision skills; for example, jumping into a business venture after the market is saturated. Not knowing the fine line

between missing the boat and sinking the ship when making important decisions, and confusing "can do" with "can't fail" in undertaking the venture, are both dangerous.

7. Many business failures are the result of partnerships gone sour. Reasons for failed partnerships include bad chemistry, personality clashes, incompatible working styles, different degrees of administrative and risk-taking ability, conflicting goals, extreme nervousness about the financial commitment (which I call "scared money"), and other unpleasant surprises partners learn about each other the hard way. At the psychological level, most real entrepreneurs can't handle partners—investors, maybe, but not partners. They inhibit each other and restrict the independence each constantly demands, needs, and thrives on. Most partnerships are doomed sooner or later.

8. Surprisingly, many businesses also fail because of early success. Once the business begins to thrive, the administrative tasks become too large for one person to handle. Unfortunately, some entrepreneurs cannot delegate. If forced to change from entrepreneurial management to the more formal "plan/organize/control" approach, they begin to feel frustrated and lose interest. Their own organizational commitment starts to decline. This can represent the beginning of the end.

9. Another serious consideration is non-acceptance by spouse and family of the abrupt change in lifestyle, the amount of time available to spend at home, and the restrictions in personal cash flow. Unfortunately, the reality of what is required to succeed in small business never fully sets in until after the venture is launched. Many times the "reality shock" of what it takes to make the business a success is too much to overcome. At that point, the venture begins a downhill slide to failure.

10. Mixing family and business relationships, with various family members taking on specific, significant responsibilities for running the business, is perhaps the most difficult challenge of all. By some estimates, only one in three family businesses survives the first generation. The primary reason for this extremely high failure rate is incompatibility of family values, which are built on unconditional love, trust, and support, with hard-nosed business principles that must focus on profitability and survival in a competitive environment.

Too often, business requirements and pressures create serious conflicts between family members that lead to destructive results. For example, it is extremely difficult to keep family matters such as sibling rivalries, boss-relative relationships, personality conflicts, financial considerations, performance appraisals, and similar issues completely separate and objective.

If you are contemplating a business venture with one or more family members playing responsible roles, be sure to forestall as many problems on the front end as possible. Preparing a detailed business plan, with all responsibilities and obligations of each family member spelled out and agreed to, is a good beginning. Pay everyone a fair wage for all work performed. Make sure all other personnel policies (titles, job descriptions, and working conditions) are handled in a professional manner. Work hard on establishing and maintaining an effective communication system. Let all family members have a say in company goals. Encourage input and feedback.

Concentrate on keeping all family matters and business issues completely separate. If serious trouble crops up, seek outside help immediately. Don't let small problems fester until they become large problems or turn into crises. This is when the business can be undermined by family-related issues.

11. Venture capitalists list other fundamental reasons for small business failure, including: a poor business plan using bad information, and possessing inadequate understanding of what it takes to succeed. Early decisions are often made without much consideration of long-term consequences. Few entrepreneurs show a willingness to formulate specific plans and stick with them. Bankers and investors then get upset. The reason? This weakness leads to other fatal problems.

12. A major question more and more would-be small business owners are asking themselves is "Should I consider franchising?" Before you leap in this direction, be sure to consult the U. S. Small Business Administration for reading materials about the advantages and pitfalls of becoming a franchisee. Do not ever sign a contract without first consulting an attorney who understands franchising law. Be sure to talk with existing franchisees about their business experience, the market potential, and (perhaps most importantly) about the integrity and support forthcoming from the franchisor. A special consideration, in addition to everything else mentioned in this chapter, is whether you have the personality to give up independence of creativity and decision-making to secure the advantages offered through the franchise agreement. Most franchise organizations have very rigid rules. Also, be very careful to determine how the franchise organization makes its money: Is it from selling franchises or from sharing the profits of franchisees? If the

franchisor does not carefully investigate you or is not willing or able to provide the training and promotion you need to be profitable, stay away.

13. Be very careful of training schools and institutes providing short-term courses designed to prepare you to enter various service businesses. Ask specific questions. First, is the industry growing? Where are investment or career opportunities located? What do future market projections indicate? What is the school's placement record? Make them document their information. Ask for references from former students and organizations hiring their graduates. Cross check their data with the U. S. Department of Labor, the U. S. Small Business Administration, national and state-level trade associations, and with individuals already in the business. Too often these training programs crop up when the field is riding a crest of growth and expansion. Remember that the next stage is product maturity, market saturation, and declining profitability, so beware! Do your homework. Do not follow the herd, and do not be seduced by seemingly glamorous career opportunities that do not exist.

14. In the years to come, one of the most frequent reasons for business failure will be employees who lack the necessary skills to do the work and who have neither the motivation nor the sense of responsibility required to deliver the service. The pool of qualified workers between the ages of 18-24 will shrink during the 1990's because of demographic trends. Troubles facing many would-be entrepreneurs will be compounded by their own shortcoming of not possessing the necessary "people leadership" qualities.

The bottom line is that too many people start a business on emotion rather than on objective market research and financial analysis. The price paid for such short-sightedness is severe. It leads not only to loss of capital or life savings, but also to the breakup of family, excessive use of alcohol or drugs, and the ultimate loss of self-esteem.

If you are contemplating answering the siren's song to independence and liberation by being your own boss, remember the genius of America is also the freedom to fail. Most small business entrepreneurs eventually do fail, at a substantial loss of money, opportunity, friendships, self-worth, and family relationships.

INFORMATION VS. EMOTION

It is absolutely essential that you do your homework. Focus on realistic planning. Get useful information to support your business plan. The Small Business Administration, local offices of state economic development agencies, Chambers of Commerce, and trade associations generally have useful material on small business. Not only should you get the material, you should also read and reflect on it. Heed it. Just as importantly, seek advice from those who have actually tried and succeeded. Talk to those who are in business and still trying. Ask those who have seen entrepreneurs win and lose, such as bankers, accountants, professional investors, and lawyers. Finally, talk to marriage and drug dependency counselors, liquidation auctioneers, and bankruptcy court clerks. Listen to what they have to say. Don't just hear what you want to hear.

DON'T OVERLOOK FAMILY

Encouragement and support from your spouse and family may be the most important success factor of all, but make sure they fully understand the odds. Spell out all the issues. Explain the track record of those who have tried before you. Make absolutely sure that all who depend on you for their lifestyle fully appreciate the magnitude of the issues involved.

Do not become a two time loser. You do not want to look back at yourself as being a failure in the corporate world and a loser in business for yourself. The price, both financially and psychologically, can be enormous.

WHAT TO DO NEXT?

If you are considering small business as an alternative to your present vocation, go into the decision with your eyes wide open. The approach to making the decision is quite simple — deal with realities! Plan, research, and deal with the facts. Harness your enthusiasm! Do not be guided by emotions or motives spawned from frustration or flowing adrenalin. Do not be controlled by the desire to be independent. Most of all, do not make your decision while running from the present. If you are bailing out, you will only increase the odds of making a bad decision.

Are you prepared to play hardball with your family savings and with your own self-esteem? It's your call. The stakes are higher than you might imagine. Remember the odds. Achieving success as a small business owner is a long shot at best. Be realistic about your chances of making it before you commit.

ENTREPRENEURSHIP CHECKLIST

- Check your motives. It's far better to move toward a new interest than to run from an old one.
- Be ready to work harder than you ever did for other people.
- Be persistent. A new business will take more time, more money, more energy than you ever thought it would.

PART IV

ACHIEVING

FULFILLMENT AND

HAPPINESS

"None but you can harm you, none but you yourself who are your greatest foe; he that respects himself is safe from others; he wears a coat of mail that none can pierce."

— Henry Wadsworth Longfellow

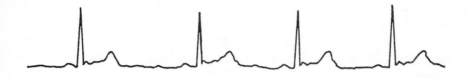

14

WHY AVOID GROWING UP?

To grow is to change. When you stop changing, you stop growing. When you stop growing, you start getting old. It's all a state of mind.

My mother was in her 70's when I broke the news to her again that for the fifth time in 25 years I was about to make a career change. I was 46 at the time.

The only question she asked still rings in my ears. *"Jim, what are you going to do when you grow up?"* As the years go by, the more I reflect on that question, the more I hope I never do grow up!

NEVER REACH THE MOUNTAIN TOP

Growing up over a lifetime, but never quite reaching the summit, is really what life is all about. When you stop growing up, you start growing old. And growing old is mostly a state of mind. To grow old is to start dying. Death of the inner spirit isn't on my list of priorities and shouldn't be on yours. People need to focus on the *growing* and downplay the "up." When you reach the "up" you have completely tested the limit of your potential. You have peaked out and have begun the journey downhill.

Instead, think of growing as a never-ending process. Set an uphill goal and approach life as an ongoing search for maturity and meaning. Experience discovery and adventure to the fullest. Come to a deeper spiritual awareness of yourself along the way.

Feeling lost as a face in the crowd, being an identification number among many, or being just another name on the roster is not where you're headed.

The key to planning and setting goals for your future is in how you value yourself as a person. Feel good about yourself. Have a strong sense of purpose and direction. They are crucial motivators. Life is an attitude and your self-worth is a barometer. What drives you and what you do with yourself comes from within. Age, circumstances, or wealth and material means don't matter that much. I've seen people who were old at 30 and others who were young at 70. Who is poor and who is rich is a matter of perception. The key to quality of life is in our goals coupled with the ability and desire to fulfill them. Are our hopes for the future brittle? Do they focus on power, authority, title, and possessions? Or do they come from the inside?

Truly happy people are those who are at peace, in control of themselves, have a balanced lifestyle, and are constantly striving to utilize their abilities and stretch themselves toward their full potential. But they have another quality: They are always sympathetic and caring about others. They like to share. They love their neighbors.

A major source of unhappiness and frustration stems from one's negative attitude about job, about self, and about position in life.

Too many people feel "boxed in" by personal circumstances or that they are captives of a lifestyle that causes them to live their lives, as Thoreau puts it, "in quiet desperation." The sad part is that quiet desperation is a sense of hopelessness and usually means that people have given up.

I have deep concern for those who feel obligated to stay with the same organization for a lifetime, even though they don't experience job satisfaction or have a sense of fulfillment. I also worry about those who fear the unknown and have no stomach to take the risks associated with responding to the dramatic changes taking place. I especially fear for those who either deny the reality of a dramatically changing world, or assume that they somehow will be safe or will always be taken care of in their job, whatever the circumstances may be. They are in for a major disappointment.

WHO SAID WE MUST?

A lot of people are simply too influenced by "bird-in-hand, depression era" values. It's baloney to believe that we owe blind loyalty to an employer simply because he was kind enough to give us a job. That attitude assumes we have done nothing worthwhile to contribute to the organization's success. This guilt-ridden attitude about jobs and careers is part of the voodoo spell the corporate medicine man seeks to cast over people. And, unfortunately, it works.

The truth is that under today's ground rules it's really okay for you to change jobs at any point in your career and feel good about the decision. Quite frankly, it may be smart thinking for you to chart a completely new course and totally change careers. Make a fresh start!

But it is very important to understand that career transitions should be the result of a personal strategic plan with a positive, unapologetic attitude. Major changes in jobs and careers don't always have to come as a result of frustration and unhappiness, reaching a dead end, or losing your job prematurely due to circumstances beyond your control. Changes should coincide with adjustments to internal values, emotional needs, spiritual and ethical beliefs, and attitudes as part of the natural maturing process we all experience. In fact, real meaning in life is discovered when we deliberately choose to change and grow, to explore new territories in life that are heretofore uncharted.

I encourage you to change jobs and change careers if that is what you want to do. More importantly, I urge you to take decisive positive steps on your own behalf if this is what you need and if you have the flexibility to do it.

Stop now and take a deep breath. Get away from the press of day-to-day routine. Think very carefully about this key point. There is absolutely no rule in the manual of life that mandates that you keep on doing what you have done in the past. Do not be hoodwinked, either by your employer or your peers, into thinking you must stay where you are. Remember, if job meltdown happens to you ... or the pink slip arrives one day ... who will be there to pick up the pieces? Only you and your family! That's who! That's why you must take control of your own destiny through career planning.

Just because you have always been an engineer, teacher, nurse, salesman, or accountant doesn't mean you are obligated to be one always. That's nonsense! You need to be what *you* want to be, tempered with what your abilities, skills, financial means, and family circumstances will permit you to be.

Or, if you have the urge and desire, but little know-how, go back to school, learn new technical skills, re-equip yourself with new job tools. Go for it!

THE ITCH TO CHANGE

There comes a point for nearly everyone where the current job or organization no longer delivers a challenge. Out of that dilemma comes a time for truth. At that moment, crucial, life-changing questions—even cries for help—come from deep within. *Am I shackled to the present? Are there other options for me? Dare I consider changing? What will my peers think? Can I afford to do it? Will my family understand? Will they support me? Where do I go from here? What must I do? What is the first step?*

If you have reached this point, are open and honest in asking questions about yourself and are seeking direction, you have already taken the first step toward a new and hopefully better future.

YOU NEED TO BE HAPPY!

Joe Barnett, author of *I Want to Be Happy*, tells us that finding real happiness in our lives is entirely up to us.[11] It is up to us not to hang our happiness on what others do or don't do, not to get hung up on circumstances, and not to let other people control us. It's our life and we have to live it our way. We need to call the shots, not let others call them for us.

Happiness begins with us and is our sole responsibility. The key to finding true happiness is to look for it in the "spiritual dimension." At this moment we can truly begin being a whole person.

LIVE FOR THE FUTURE!

My publisher John Ishee observed that people sometimes "seek security at the expense of happiness. When they find a comfortable niche in life, they settle in and begin spending their energies defending where they are rather than continuing to grow. But this is self-defeating, and the fruit of this approach is the seed of despair."[12] Since life is never static, but is constantly in process, any person who seeks to maintain the status quo by living in the present ends up missing the joy and challenge of living in the future.

We should never become trapped by the uncomfortable and meaningless cycle of non-growth. The answer, according to Ishee, lies in our personal value system. We must place priority upon our commitment to be a growing person. Growing, then, becomes the organizing principle around which we build our lives.

Because of these reasons, I encourage you to keep drawing closer to that spiritual base, to keep questioning life's purpose, to seek honest answers from a spiritual perspective, to seek "wholeness" and balance in your life, to become more strategic about your career and, if possible in terms of need, skills, and family circumstances, to begin charting a new course, or to put to rest, once and for all, the uneasiness you feel and go on with what you are, where you are. Sooner or later you must be at peace with yourself so you can be happy. If you are not happy, you are nothing—you are nowhere—so do whatever is required to come to grips with being happy.

If happiness in a career requires that you increase your capacity for doing a job and you aren't willing to pay the price, then admit it. Or if you aren't willing or able to make the adjustments required, then resolve the internal conflict and accept your present situation as your final destination. Serenity comes from peace within yourself.

Far too many people work entire careers being unhappy and unfulfilled. They don't seem to know what they want to do, where they want to go, or even what is happening to them. And even if they do, they don't feel confident of their skills or do not have the personal courage, family support, or financial resources to do anything positive and constructive to resolve their dilemma.

As a result, they continue in their careers, becoming increasingly dissatisfied to the point of misery. At that crossroads, if nothing is done to change and seek relief, they become an empty shell and start to die from within.

This is tragic because our goal always ought to be to press forward to seek the limits of our inner power and to find opportunities to test these limits, to stretch them and utilize our potential to the fullest. We never get too old for the experience, even in retirement.

Remember that it is never too late to take full control. Even if you are nearing retirement, you can still review where you are, ask important questions, and do strategic planning for the future. At every stage, you need to use your time productively and in pursuits which you enjoy and which give you fulfillment. It's your life. You need to make absolutely sure you live it on your own terms all the way.

How old are you? 30? 40? 50? You may have 20, 30, or 40 years of productive life ahead of you. Be prepared to live them to the fullest. Remember that your career is always in process. Nothing is ever locked in or guaranteed. Through self-management, you must take charge of yourself and those who depend on you.

REMEMBER ALICE JENKINS!

Don't kid yourself—no one else can or will do your planning for you. It's entirely up to you. Not only must you have a plan, you must take the important step of putting your plan to work, and stick with it. This is where most of us fail. We have good intentions but cannot deliver. We procrastinate. Always meaning to live, we never live with meaning. Don't be guilty of this destructive trait. Don't be like Alice Jenkins (of Chapter Five) and be remembered only as a person who "existed."

After you set your goals and establish priorities, press on. Above all, remember the proverb "happiness is a journey, not a destination." As Joe Barnett tells us, "happiness is found in the pursuit—not just in achievement." Always grow toward "up"— but never get there. Avoid the downhill slide. If you find yourself at the top, set new goals and climb even higher.

I've discovered there is life after 20, after 30, after 40, and after 50. It just keeps getting better at every stage. I still seek new mountains to climb. Come join me on the journey toward self-fulfillment and happiness. With God's help, after 50 years, the pursuit has just begun.

GROWTH CHECKLIST

- Examine your attitude toward change. Are you adjusting to new situations or defending old ones?
- Make a list of eight or ten values you either possess or desire to possess. How does your present career situation reflect these values?
- Do something each day to contribute to your growth.

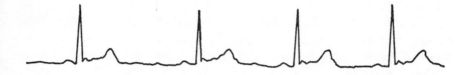

15

DRAWING ON BASIC BELIEFS AND SPIRITUAL VALUES

Too many are caught in life's activity and lose out on life's meaning. If we expect nothing of ourselves, or set our sights too low, we are telling ourselves we aren't worth much. That's sad. But there is an answer.

After thirty years of observing people and studying organizations, I am firmly convinced that two of our country's greatest wastes are unfulfilled potential and lost opportunity -- not only for individuals and businesses, but also for families, churches, communities, governments, and societies.

WHY WE FALL SHORT

Why do we squander potential and miss opportunity? Why do we fall short of our capacity in pursuit of goals and objectives? The reason goes back to the central theme of this book: *We aren't in charge.* Far too many of us let things happen *to* us rather than make things happen *for* us. We refuse to accept responsibility for ourselves, our careers, and what's important to us. We mistakenly assume that somebody else—our bosses, supervisors, or employers—will take care of us.

In determining what is important to us and how we relate to others, we rely too much on the values of humanism and the pleasures of materialism. We focus on today and let tomorrow fend for itself. Having all the answers, we don't draw enough on spiritual values for guidance.

We feel little ownership or responsibility for the world around us. We have an insufficient stewardship commitment to the public institutions which are vital to our future well-being. We forget our obligation to protect the environment and resources for the benefit of future generations. We place too much emphasis on "me" and "now" in the yuppie generation sense. We have the same short-term pragmatism in our personal lives that has befallen business and industry. We are unwilling to look or to plan ahead. Our main concern is today instead of tomorrow. We take from society, but don't give back to the community. We operate under the delusion that life is a stable, predictable course, always onward and upward. In reality, life is a series of stages and cycles, each containing adjustments, uncertainties, surprises, disruptions, endings, and new beginnings.

Many of us don't have the self-awareness, self-discipline, or self-confidence required to take full command of ourselves as we travel life's journey. We simply wander along with the tide of affairs, missing the new and fresh experiences available to us. We never realize that the *real key* to achieving career success and personal happiness comes *from deep within*. We often fall short of where we need to be or how to go on with our lives. Not being alert or able to make choices, we struggle along at half-speed and miss opportunities. Life eventually becomes dull and uninteresting, filled with clutter and nothingness. Bad things tend to sneak up on us, and we are hounded economically, emotionally, and spiritually. Instead of positive growth experiences, unpleasant setbacks happen to us throughout our career. In Shakespeare's words:

> To-morrow, and to-morrow, and to-morrow,
> creeps on this petty pace from day to day
> To the last syllable of recorded time;
> And all our yesterdays have lighted fools
> The way to dusty death, Out, out brief candle!
> Life's but a walking shadow, a poor player
> That struts and frets his hour upon the stage

And then is heard no more: it is a tale
Told by an idiot, full of sound and fury,
Signifying nothing.

A major reason for increased alcohol abuse, drug usage, and sadness is that we don't have enough *self-esteem*. We question our significance as individuals. We don't value ourselves very highly. Being second best and mediocre are becoming acceptable. Doing it only if it's easy or absolutely necessary is becoming the norm. Our leaders don't reinforce the need for pride or encourage us to do more than what is required. We don't reinforce or encourage one another to excel, to stretch ourselves. Choosing to go it alone, we *don't have support groups to bolster us during times of need.* Behind the cheerful mask our pride forces us to wear is far too much frustration, emptiness, loneliness, and crying deep within. Unfortunately, most of the reasons for these afflictions are self-imposed. But they can be prevented or, at least, minimized.

WHAT DO YOU STAND FOR?

At the bottom of all this frustration is a lack of basic beliefs. We simply do not know what we believe. We don't determine our basic values. We don't make commitments. We don't take firm stands. Most of us have a hunger for recognition and achievement, a desire to be noticed, and a need for acceptance that too often controls our thoughts and our actions. But we don't know how to deal with it all or really how to understand the time and emotional energy these demands take. We are weakened and victimized by peer pressure or are overly influenced by unhealthy social trends. We signify nothing of our own making or choosing. We simply follow the herd. We haven't defined clear-cut ethical limits to our behavior or determined minimum standards of conduct we will accept from others.

The problem is that we haven't tapped into the sources of spiritual help available to us. Our spiritual awareness remains at a superficial level. We don't take full advantage of the fruit of the Spirit: love, joy, peace, patience, kindness, goodness, faithfulness, gentleness, and self-control. We don't unlock the real secret to peace of mind, contentment, and purpose for vital living recorded in biblical scriptures. We suffer and flounder as a direct result. This is so sad and unnecessary.

We all have the intellect to deal with life's economic, physiological, emotional, and spiritual issues, but we don't put these resources to work. We don't use our brains. We are mentally lazy, lacking the toughness and firmness of judgment necessary to deal with problems in a thoughtful and decisive manner. Caught up in life's daily activity, we lose out on life's real meaning. Because of this flaw, we miss growth opportunities available at each stage of our career. The end result is that we don't operate close to our mental, physical, and spiritual potential.

TIME FOR SELF-EXAMINATION

As you think about family, friends, community, government, and social causes, do you know what is really important to you? If you had to sit down and make a priority list of ways in which you actually apply your talents and energies, would you be on target? Or would your actions and activities on the one hand, and priorities and aspirations on the other, appear like ships passing in the night?

One of my favorite poems is Robert Frost's "The Road Not Taken:"

> Two roads diverged in a yellow wood,
> And sorry I could not travel both
> And be one traveler, long I stood
> And looked down one as far as I could
> To where it bent in the undergrowth;
> Then took the other, as just as fair,
> And having perhaps the better claim,
> Because it was grassy and wanted wear;
> Though as for that the passing there
> Had worn them really about the same,
> And both that morning equally lay
> In leaves no step had trodden black.
> Oh, I kept the first for another day!
> Yet knowing how way leads on to way,
> I doubted I should ever come back.
> I shall be telling this with a sigh
> Somewhere ages and ages hence:

Two roads diverged in a wood, and I --
I took the one less traveled by,
And that has made all the difference.[13]

We are challenged by Frost to decide for ourselves whether we will put our future—our life—in our own hands rather than allow others to take control. The decision rests in the choice of roads we take: the well-worn road of the crowd leading to conformity, or the untrampled road leading to individualism and personal satisfaction.

SETTING LIFE'S PRIORITIES

Nemiwashi! This Japanese principle translates to solid advice for each of us. *It means tending to the roots*, going back to basics, sticking with the fundamentals, not letting life get too complicated or trying to do too much, utilizing our personal resources wisely, setting priorities, focusing on what is really important, having the courage to withstand the pressures of those who wish to rob our success and happiness, not wasting ourselves on meaningless activity, understanding the positive energizing sources of inner power available in our lives, knowing where we can get the real strength to overcome adversity and hardship, and finally mustering courage to take the steps into uncertainty and ambiguity, often at great perceived risk, required to reach the potential of our God-given talents.

Here are five suggestions for taking charge of who you are. They will help you to understand the starting point, to determine where you want to go, to assess the cost of getting there, and to realize fully the consequences of not taking the necessary actions required.

1. *Believe That Life Has A Purpose For You.* Be confident that you are important and have value as a human being. To build on this principle you must know your strengths and weaknesses. I'm talking about a self-appraisal of talents, skills, brains, personality, capabilities, traits, and physical strength. Honestly identify your abilities and shortcomings. Lay out the facts. This requires forthrightness and a willingness to come to grips with who and what you really are. This is second-stage maturity in action (as discussed in Chapter Five).

But there is more. In order to apply your talents, you have to match your internal strengths and personal weaknesses with the personal growth and career building opportunities available to you. At the same time, potential threats to your job readiness and economic well-being must be identified. These include such possibilities as technological obsolescence, employee cutbacks, or other negative circumstances impacting job security or job happiness resulting from bad working conditions or poor leadership. Business planners call this management tool a situational or "SWOT" (strengths, weaknesses, opportunities, and threats) analysis. Utilize this helpful business approach to conduct your own candid examination of yourself and how you fit into your world. It's a crucial first step in personal strategic planning.

2. *Work On Setting A Few Goals.* Most people live to obtain goals. Goal-setting fosters the self-discipline required for a person to take mental and physical steps in a new direction. If goals are reasonable, challenging, manageable, time-bound, and obtainable, they offer fresh hope and inspiration. Goals help us see a vision for ourselves. This leads to new excitement and enthusiasm.

Most people fail to understand the key principle that goals become our personal worth. If we set our sights too low, we are telling ourselves that we aren't worth very much. If we expect nothing out of ourselves, or give little of ourselves, we assume we won't be disappointed in ourselves. But eventually we are disappointed—we tend to achieve at our own level of expectation, which is often below the potential of our ability.

At some point in our careers, we each need to experience the refreshing, and often exhilerating adventure of making fresh tracks in new snow instead of always just following a tried and established trail. Therefore, it is vitally important that this goal-setting issue be dealt with on a regular basis.

Why not try setting some specific, simple, short term, attainable goals? Focus on them. Review progress. Make adjustments when necessary. When you achieve a goal, set your sights higher. Keep growing.

3. *Review Personal Circumstances Regularly.* Self-examination and goal-setting become especially crucial at key crossroads or "crisis points" in our lives. These "crisis points" include experiencing the first job, getting married, raising teen-agers, discovering ourselves in mid-career, seeing retirement on our horizon, and approaching the later years. There will also be unexpected times which require setting the personal planning process in motion once more—examples are job loss,

boredom, career burnout, financial crisis, major illness, divorce, and other family-related setbacks.

It is for these reasons that personal goal-setting, planning, and evaluation must become a life-long process. Not only should we plan and set new goals as personal circumstances change, we must also have the courage and sense of timing to put the new plan to work. If we decide to do something different, we must follow through. This last step is generally where we fall short. We have good intentions, but weaken at the moment of truth. We don't implement. This flaw can contribute to our economic and emotional undoing.

4. *Answer Some Tough Questions About Yourself.* A genuinely mature person is honest. If I'm not happy, whose fault is that? If my work life, home life, or social life, marriage or career are sagging, have I really tried? Have I gone at least halfway to make it work? Am I really committed? Have I been an instrument of change for the better? Am I the solution, or have I actually been the problem by being selfish, self-centered, angry, unwilling to negotiate, unable to communicate, inflexible, willing to compromise to gain unfair advantage, or unwilling to accept responsibility for making things better? In short, have I been failing to take charge of the situation? Have I failed to demonstrate the positive leadership required to set things right?

Where do you stack up on this critical scale of spiritual maturity/immaturity?

5. *Check Yourself For Balance.* Do you really work to improve yourself physically, mentally, philosophically, economically, and spiritually? Providing this balance is a huge responsibility. But these five dimensions of life are the cues for determining your strong points, your weaknesses, and knowing where you are now in terms of what is most important to you. You should not play down or exclude any of these personal dimensions. Deal with each one as you seek new meaning for yourself at every career stage. It may be that you focus too much on money, lifestyle, or material possessions while giving little, if any, thought to your inner character and basic beliefs. In short, you may be driven by externally imposed goals rather than by internal values. Many people who crash at mid-life suffer from an unbalanced view of what is important and what isn't. They become losers because they have no concept of the true spiritual meaning of life.

For example, our drive for career advancement and material success can cause us to make decisions that come back to visit us later as we begin to consider life in more philosophical terms. As we move through the 30's and 40's, we begin to look in the mirror and come to realize the earlier career short cuts have tarnished our feeling of self-worth. We also see we have compromised our integrity. These feelings begin to haunt us. Life at this crossroads becomes a monumental moment of truth. How we come to grips with our emotions and resolve them becomes very crucial to continued growth toward emotional and spiritual maturity.

When all is said and done, an adult simply cannot find true success and happiness in life "going it" alone, ignoring the issue of spirituality in the process. The question of who is in charge of our lives must be addressed sooner or later if one's full potential as a spiritual person is to be achieved.

POWER OVER SELF

After the Orbiter *Challenger* exploded, a commentator observed that with all the emphasis on space stations, Star Wars, and planet colonies, we are missing the real frontier—"inner space." This vast interior inside ourselves from which we draw to achieve our goals, reach new heights, and take new direction can go virtually untapped. I call it inner power.

It's amazing to me how much inner power each of us has available to help us do whatever we desire, if only we would use it. In assessing this internal energy source, do we fully understand that our lives are our responsibility and opportunity? Our actions are our exclusive choice. Coming to this realization is the first crucial step toward tapping the energy source that exists within each of us.

Do we appreciate the obligation we have to know ourselves, to determine assets as well as shortcomings? Are we willing to overcome our weaknesses, to fully develop ourselves, and to nurture our relationships with others? We should never forget that regardless of age, experience, wealth, or position, it is always the right time to stop and take a hard and honest look inward to determine the right course. See whether the things that turn you on and the lifestyle you support provide a genuine satisfaction and a deep sense of fulfillment.

AT PEACE WITH OURSELVES

The toughest stage to achieve in life is reaching the point where we can be totally honest and be totally happy with ourselves at the same time. The acid test of this accomplishment is to reach deep within our souls on a daily basis. And if during these quiet times, when we reflect on our lives, our deeds, actions, motives, thoughts, and words, we really are at peace with ourselves, then we have arrived at perhaps life's most important destination ... spiritual maturity.

My challenge to you is this: If you are to have a happy, meaningful life, with inner peace of mind in the deepest spiritual sense, you must do three things.

1. Make absolutely certain your life's priorities are firmly entrenched in ethical, spiritual beliefs. If your life is to be successful you must have real purpose. Have something important to live for, something significant to grow toward. If you haven't dealt with this issue, work on it now. Set your goals and objectives accordingly. *Take command!*

2. Take full responsibility for who you are. Answer this question: have you accepted full accountability for your own economic, physical, and moral well-being? If you haven't, start now to do this. *Take control!*

3. Know fully and honestly what abilities, traits, and qualities you have within you as you begin to grow. Then decide what you are going to do to get better. Always dwell on strengths. *Take charge!*

WHERE TO BEGIN

Most of us can go much further, much faster, and with more excitement, achievement, and fulfillment in our lives if we will unleash that hidden, pent-up inner power.

But obstacles get in the way. Some are beyond our control, but most are within our grasp. Here's a partial list of typical barriers to personal growth:

1. Lack of personal discipline
2. Lack of self-confidence and self-worth
3. Lack of willpower and self-control
4. Laziness
5. Passiveness

6. Procrastination

7. A willingness to let somebody else do it

8. Fear of change and resistance to new ways and procedures

9. Thoughtlessness: It didn't come to mind or didn't occur to me that I could do it

10. No excitement or desire to gain new information about things important to well-being

11. No leadership from others

12. No reinforcement for a job well done

13. Fear of peers

14. Intellectual dishonesty, bad habits, or poor ethics

15. No goals; therefore, no sense of achievement

OTHER SELF-INFLICTED WOUNDS

We also let ourselves be victimized by resentment, anger, frustration, guilt, envy, and hatred for others. These feelings gain control over our thoughts and our actions. They distract us, drain our energy, waste our brainpower, and sap the strength we need to move forward and pursue objectives. This is automatic self-destruction.

We must deal with unresolved conflicts, personality clashes, and other barriers to inner peace and joy to fully tap the potential contained within us. Otherwise, we aren't fulfilling our obligation to ourselves.

ACCEPTING RESPONSIBILITY FOR HEALING

We need an escape valve. To begin with, we must stop leaning on our own understanding. Instead, we must draw on spiritual strength for guidance in coming to grips with problems we all have, especially when dealing with others.

Here again, we must ask ourselves the following question: Are we the problem? Do we practice forgiveness? Do we have the ability to control anger? To turn the other cheek? To take the first step in putting the past behind us? And as a last resort, remove ourselves from the situation permanently?

Once we have identified the negatives that influence our attitudes or take control of our actions, we must move decisively to eliminate them. We must take them on, one by one, and then fill each vacuum with something positive instead. This is the way to steer a proper course toward the goals and opportunities important in achieving a more meaningful life.

WE ALSO NEED GOD'S POWER

Ralph Keys wrote, "My realization that I'll never solve all my own problems, let alone the world's, seems to be the beginning of wisdom." Catherine Marshall tells us that, "There is a great maturity in being helpless." The message of both statements is to turn to God for the answers.

To reach the heights in life and overcome the difficulties we face, we must look beyond our own abilities and not rely on our own achievements. Being dependent upon God as the source of our spiritual strength, whatever the circumstances, deals a mortal blow to the most serious sin of all: attempting to go through life totally relying on our own resources.

As the message on a church marquee once read: "If you love money you will never be satisfied by it." It's this way with most of our concerns, but by linking our internal battery to the ultimate power source we can be on the way to achieving what matters most: inner joy and peace, coupled with hope and anticipation of good things to come. If not in this life, we find it in the life we have been promised if we accept the gift offered by God. The beauty of it is that all He expects from us is our willingness to let Him work through us—for our own good!

THE WINNING COMBINATION

The 19th century protestant preacher Henry Ward Beecher wrote: "Every tomorrow has two handles: We can take hold of it with the handle of anxiety and uncertainty or the handle of faith and confidence." Nothing has really changed in 100 years. Each person in every generation has the same choice to make. This decision is ours. The key is in having the confidence in ourselves, based on personal strengths and basic beliefs, while drawing heavily on unwavering faith in a Superior Being. This is the real winning combination.

BASIC BELIEFS CHECKLIST

- Review what's important to you—your priorities. What you stand for, if anything.
- Identify your basic beliefs. Do you have any? One way to do this is to write them down. Don't stop to evaluate them at first—just get them down on paper. Then refine and evaluate them.
- Develop a belief system to guide you in personal and workplace decision-making.
- Implement your system of basic beliefs.
- Stay with these beliefs. Rely on them. Be guided by them always.
- If you have difficulty in identifying basic beliefs or struggle with the concept of spirituality, begin now exploring ways to overcome this barrier to inner peace and true fulfillment.
- Make a commitment to try.
- Do not be too hard on yourself in the process.
- Begin by setting goals, believing in yourself, and feeling good about yourself.
- Seek out a support group to help you with this issue.
- Start today.

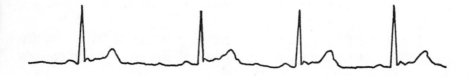

16

GETTING ON WITH YOUR CAREER

Too many people have hopes and dreams, but never do anything about them. They have good motives, but are not motivated. They never put good intentions into action. If you don't make your career work for you, life's circumstances will work against you.

My teen-age daughter, Sally, came up with a marvelous original thought. She posed this question: "How do you determine the color of your brain?" The answer: "By the pigment of your imagination!"

My question is similar. What is the color of *your* brain? Has the message of this book stirred the pigment of *your* imagination? Are you challenged to take the no-nonsense steps required to gain full control of your career, and to make whatever plans and to pursue all actions necessary to ensure that you remain in charge of your future?

A major reason so many people are unhappy today is that they suffer from a sometimes fatal flaw: They have hopes and dreams, but never do anything about them. They have high aspirations, but do nothing to make them a reality. They have good motives, but are not motivated to action. They never put their good intentions to work. Instead of making their careers work for them, they let life's circumstances work against them. As a result, they are victimized by their self-inflicted failures.

Please do not let this self-imposed malady of inaction and paralysis be your undoing. If you now live in a comfort zone (have a good job, feel warmly secure, are told regularly how wonderful everything is, and are settled into life's routine), beware of corporate seduction and voodoo.

Understand that you could become a victim of "obsolescence shock." Someday you could be fired or laid off from your job for reasons totally out of your control. My advice is that, while you live in the present, always keep attuned to the future. Do not live in the past or spend vital energy longing for seemingly better days in a modern day Garden of Eden that will never return.

Instead, maintain yourself in a state of preparedness and readiness. Make absolutely sure you are on firm footing in terms of the stability of your employer and the strength of your job skills and marketability. If it becomes necessary, be able to move from where you are now to where you need to go. Let life work for you as much as possible and on your own timetable.

SINCERITY ISN'T ENOUGH!

In an uncertain world, do not be lulled into thinking that good things will automatically happen to you, especially if you press your shoulder to the wheel, work hard, are nice to your boss, and keep your nose clean. It just doesn't work that way anymore. This is not a fairy tale. It's cold reality.

To achieve success, you must follow the principles of career self-management: assessment of career preferences and personal capability; self-improvement; moral, emotional, spiritual, and physical fitness; personal strategic planning; financial flexibility; investing in your own knowledge and then investing that knowledge in yourself.

The framework for living with meaning, achieving career success, and finding personal happiness based on your goals is in:

1. Accepting full responsibility for yourself, your personal well-being, and that of those who depend on you—*BEING READY!*

2. Developing the right attitude, having the motivation to take charge, and having the courage to act—*BEING WILLING!*

3. Having the necessary job skills, flexibility, and mobility to go where the jobs are—*BEING ABLE!*

4. Actually taking the first step by overcoming the first hurdle of inaction—*DOING IT!*

"IF IT IS TO BE, IT'S UP TO ME"

When all is said and done, life's major decisions are up to you. The responsibility for achieving what you want from a career, and in life, is yours alone. Will you accept this challenge and take charge of your personal destiny? Will you do whatever is required to rise to your full potential of mind, body, and spirit as a human being? Whatever your circumstances, your age, or your location, I urge you to do so ... and to begin your journey now. Take the road less traveled by. It will make all the difference.

CAREER PLANNING CHECKLIST

- Face change. Rapid change is a reality.
- Take charge. Manage your career. Remember that no one else can do it for you to your satisfaction.
- Stay in control. Don't abdicate your responsibilities.
- Work smart at every stage. Keep abreast of job trends.
- Remember—your goal is to achieve fulfillment and happiness. Make decisions based on this goal.

NOTES

1. Theodore Levitt, "Marketing Myopia," Harvard Business Review (July-August, 1960) and "Retrospective Commentary," *Harvard Business Review* (September-October, 1975).

2. Ross Campbell, *How To Really Love Your Teenager* (Wheaton, IL: Victor Books, 1982), p. 73.

3. For ideas concerning the types of companies that are doing it right (and wrong) see for example: Richard Foster, *Innovations* (New York: Summitt Books, 1986); Frederick Betz, *Managing Technology* (Englewood Cliffs: Prentice-Hall, Inc., 1987); and Thomas S. Peters and Robert N. Waterman, Jr., *In Search of Excellence* (New York: Harper and Row, Publishers, Inc.,1982).

4. Douglas LaBier, *Modern Madness: The Emotional Fallout of Success* (Reading, MA: Addison-Wesley, 1987).

5. See Fred Smith, *You and Your Network* (Waco: Word Books, 1984) for ideas on networking and mentoring. Listening to his wisdom will tempt anyone to pursue excellence.

6. David Crosby, *People Weekly*, April 27, 1987, p. 454.

7. Credit is given to Gerald O'Collins, *The Second Journey* (New York: Paulist Press, 1978) for several ideas contained in this chapter.

8. The idea for chapter 11 (and some of the information included) came from unpublished materials by Auzville Jackson, Jr., patent attorney and former corporate executive who served as the first president and CEO of the Tennessee Technology Foundation, Oak Ridge, Tennessee.

9. Credit is given to the Carnegie Corporation; Alan Pifer and D. Lydia Bronte; and Teachers Insurance and Annuity Association, New York for the information used in this section. The material was taken from *Research Dialogues*, issue number 14, a publication of TIAA/CREF. It came originally from *Our Aging Society: Paradox and Promise*, published as a Carnegie Corporation sponsored study. Pifer was the project chairman. Bronte was staff director.

10. Ibid.

11. Joe R. Barnett, *I Want To Be Happy* (Lubbock: Pathway Publishing House, Inc., 1983).

12. John A. Ishee, *From Here To Maturity* (Brentwood, TN: J M Productions, Inc., 1985).

13. *The Complete Poems of Robert Frost* (New York: Holt, Rinehart, and Winston, 1964), p. 131 (used by permission).

Appendix: Value Of Three-Year Career Reviews

●<u>Stop at least every three years and carefully assess where you are
in your career and where you are headed.</u> Are you where you want to
be? Are you moving in the right direction? Do you know where you
want to go and how to get there? If not, deal with these issues. Don't
sweep them under the rug. Do something constructive to get yourself
on course and keep yourself there. The future has a far better chance
of happening for you if you focus your efforts on the present, not where
you hope to be 10 to 15 years from now. Don't make the mental leap
from where you are now in your career to your ultimate goal, bypassing
several vital steps of preparation in the process.

Living too far ahead involves too much wishful thinking, causes
loss of concentration, and results in the waste of valuable time. The out-
come can be too much false hope, too many empty dreams, and, ultimately, career disappointment.

●<u>Always keep in mind that your current job is a necessary step in
career progress — a time of discovery and preparation.</u> You are learning about yourself: What you like and dislike about job content,
workplace rules, people with whom you associate, timetables and dead-
lines, problems and pressures, disappointments and achievements.

Every job situation is a unique building block — and opportunity
for seasoning. You are preparing your resumé each step of the way.
Most importantly, you are learning about yourself: Who you really are
and what you really want out of life, in the real world of work.

The fundamental reason why you shouldn't aim your thoughts and
dreams too far ahead of where you are now is that your future is largely unpredictable. Too many things can happen, and likely will happen,
both good and bad, to change the course of your career.

● <u>An early career lesson is the realization that things are not always as they seem.</u> Often, there is a sizable negative gap between expectations (what you hope for) and cold reality (what you actually get).
It is important that you do your homework and deal with facts, not emotions.

Job circumstances and work conditions change. Industries and professions experience transitions. Technologies and skills required to do the work shift. Bosses come and go. Companies are bought and sold. People you depend on can't always deliver or don't always follow through. Your vocational interests and personal needs can change. You also will likely change as you experience a variety of job and interpersonal relationships, and as you grow in years.

Because of all these reasons and the uncertainties of life, no one can, with any degree of confidence, look more than three years down the road. It's best to concentrate on the present, using the time to develop your skills. Observe what you like best and dislike most about your work and about yourself. Since the future is unpredictable, opportunities can and will present themselves. Unforeseen barriers and obstacles to continued career progress, some of your own making and some outside your control, can and will crop up.

• The secret is to take control and always stay in charge. Remain alert and be flexible. Always be totally honest with yourself. Do you have what it takes to achieve what you want? What are your strengths and weaknesses? Are you willing to pay the price? Never assume that someone else is looking after your career interests or that somehow good things will automatically happen. Neither assume that career is a steady course — onward and upward — nor that the future will take care of itself. Don't be victimized by career shock.

• Keep in mind that success is getting what you want; happiness is wanting what you get. The objective of every career self-manager should be to have the wisdom to know the difference. If so, the result is more likely to be the measure of personal fulfillment that you seek.

• Make your career happen for you ... not to you. The bottom line in career management is this: Whatever your goal, achievement is ultimately up to you.

• Have a vision for yourself, but keep it in perspective. Set your sights on rising to your full potential and having the opportunity to do so. Make your own career breaks. Patience and self-discipline are required. You must also have the courage and financial means to make your dreams a reality. In the progress of career growth, you get from here to there three years at a time.

ABOUT THE AUTHOR

The author, Dr. James C. Cotham, III, is currently Graduate Professor of Management Strategy and Policy at the Jack C. Massey Graduate School of Business, Belmont College, Nashville, Tennessee. In addition, he is an independent management consultant, specializing in strategic planning, leadership, organizational problems, and human resources development.

Private Sector

Cotham spent nearly 10 years in the private sector in a variety of executive-level positions. He was Vice President for Administrative and Customer Services with the Nashville Gas Company, an investor-owned gas distribution utility; General Manager, business marketing, South Central Bell; Senior Vice President of Marketing, Nashville City Bank; and President and Chief Operating Officer, First National Bank, Clarksville, Tennessee.

Government Service

Cotham served for more than three years in the cabinet of Governor Lamar Alexander as Commissioner of Economic and Community Development for the State of Tennessee. In this capacity, he gained experience in the world arena by direct contact with businesses, both locally and internationally, in the areas of industrial development, community planning, and existing industry programs.

One of the highlights of this executive assignment was serving as coordinator for the project which successfully recruited the massive Nissan Motor Manufacturing Company to a location near Nashville, Tennessee. This was widely regarded as a major industrial coup, and opened the door for further industrial development of this type in the region.

Teaching, Research, Administration

In terms of higher education, Cotham has 18 years of experience in teaching, research, and administration. While at the University of Tennessee, he was Professor of Marketing, Associate Dean of the College of Business Administration, Director of Executive Development Programs, and Director for the Center for Business and Economic Research. Cotham is a former member of the State University Board of Regents, serving as Chairman of the Academic programs and Policies Committee. He has also served as Adjunct Professor in the Owen Graduate School of Management, Vanderbilt University. A frequent speaker to civic, business, and professional groups, Cotham has published 25 articles and monographs dealing with business and public policy issues.

Cotham is on the Board of Directors of the Tennessee Technological Foundation, an organization working to promote high technology industry on a state-wide basis. He has also been active on projects designed to reduce adult illiteracy, improve basic job skills, and assist schools to set goals for the future. Recognized for his planning skills, Cotham was the recipient in 1981 of the first annual "Excellence in Planning" Award by the Planning Executives Institute. In 1977, he was named "Communicator of the Year" by the Middle Tennessee Chapter of the Public Relations Society of America.

Educational Background

Cotham graduated from Austin Peay State University in 1957 with a B.S. degree in Business Administration. As a student at APSU, he was class President during his freshman and senior years, and received the Drane Award as outstanding graduate. In 1959, he received his M.S. degree from the University of Tennessee-Knoxville, majoring in Marketing and Economics. At UT, Cotham was elected to the Beta Gamma Sigma and Phi Kappa Phi national scholastic honor societies.

Cotham attended the Graduate School of Business at Indiana University, receiving the Doctor of Business Administration degree in 1967. Fields of study included marketing, personnel and organizational behavior, psychology, economics, and transportation. While at Indiana University, he was named Eastman Kodak Fellow.

Cotham has been listed in Outstanding Young Men of America by the National Junior Chamber of Commerce and is an honorary member of Delta Sigma Phi and Alpha Kappa Phi national business fraternities. Active in civic work, Cotham has served as a board member and officer for a variety of charitable organizations. He and his family are members of the United Methodist Church where he has served as lay leader, Sunday school teacher, and in the work areas of family life, stewardship, evangelism, finance, and parish-staff relations.